POST-
REVOLUTIONARY
SOCIETY

POST-REVOLUTIONARY SOCIETY

essays by Paul M. Sweezy

Monthly Review Press
New York and London

Library of Congress Cataloging in Publication Data
Sweezy, Paul Marlor, 1910-
    Post-revolutionary society.
    Includes bibliographical references.
    CONTENTS: Lessons of the Soviet experience.—
Lessons of Poland.—Transition to socialism. [etc.]
    1. Russia—Social conditions—1917-
2. Social classes—Russia.   3. Socialism.
4. Socialism in Russia.   5. Socialism in China.
I. Title.
HN526.S9   947.084   80-8085
ISBN 0-85345-550-3

Monthly Review Press
62 West 14th Street, New York, N.Y. 10011
47 Red Lion Street, London, WC1R 4 PF

Manufactured in the United States of America

10 9 8 7 6 5 4 3 2 1

For Zirel

CONTENTS

PREFACE

The twentieth century may well go down in history as the century of revolutions. First there was the Russian Revolution, affecting what in territorial terms is by far the largest country in the world. This revolution spread to Eastern Europe in the wake of the Red Army in the last phase of World War II, much as the French Revolution was extended to parts of Western Europe by Napoleon's armies in the preceding century. Next came the Chinese Revolution, the culmination of a century-long struggle in the world's most populous country. Other post-World War II revolutions have taken place in Indochina, Korea, Cuba, Portugal's former African colonies, the Horn of Africa, and most recently Southern Yemen, Iran, and Nicaragua. All in all, so far this century, about 30 percent of the earth's land area and 35 percent of its population have gone through revolutions involving profound structural changes. And all the indications are that the final two decades of the century will witness a continuation and perhaps even an acceleration of this process. No previous century has experienced anything remotely comparable to these enormous upheavals and transformations.

What kind of society are these revolutions creating?

Most have triumphed under the banner of Marxism, and (with the notable exception of the Iranian Revolution) the rest have espoused Marxism (or Marxism-Leninism) soon after the conquest of power. Since Marxism has always taught that the successor to capitalism would be socialism, it is natural that these revolutionary societies should call themselves socialist. And it is also natural that bourgeois social science, which never anticipated or attempted to explain these revolutions as other than historical accidents, should accept the socialist label even while often interpreting it in ways quite unacceptable to the revolutionary regimes themselves.

If we probe more deeply, we find that the founders of Marxism—Karl Marx himself and his close co-worker Friedrich Engels—carefully refrained from offering any blueprints of the socialist society of the future, and in fact where they discussed its characteristics at all they treated it as a transitional society between capitalism and communism (which they regarded as the ultimate goal toward which history was moving).

Given this background, it is not surprising that there has never been a consensus among Marxists, and still less among anti-Marxists or non-Marxists, about what an actual socialist society would or ought to look like. The result is that the term has come to be used simply as a convenient label for all the revolutionary societies which apply it to themselves, while everyone, friend and foe alike, is free to interpret it in whatever way seems most useful or convenient.

This situation is of course not unique to socialism. There are many other terms in common use which are interpreted very differently by different groups or individuals: freedom, democracy, development, progress, and many more. Each has its history and its power to evoke a variety of responses. We all use them—to communicate, to persuade, to stimulate to action. But when the object is to explain or understand a phenomenon or process—which I take to be the general purpose of the sciences—we had better use terms like these only in ways that do not leave them open to a wide range of interpretations. This is why, in analyzing the societies which have been created by the revolutions of the twentieth century, I have used the term socialism sparingly and only where I think the context makes the meaning unambiguously clear. In particular I have not adopted the common practice of calling all these societies socialist, but instead have used the neutral and purely descriptive term "post-revolutionary."

After what has been said about the scope and number of revolutions in our time and the likelihood that more are in the offing, I hardly need to urge on the reader the importance of the subject itself. Whether I have succeeded in throwing light on it is another question: readers will have to decide that for themselves.

My intellectual debts, apart from those which appear in the text, are primarily to the remarkable group of comrades and co-workers I have been fortunate enough to be associated with in the three decades I have devoted mainly to *Monthly Review* and Monthly Review Press: Leo Huberman and Paul Baran, Harry Magdoff and Harry Braverman, and most recently Jules Geller. I don't know to what extent the ideas put forward here are originally theirs, nor how far they do, or would if they were still alive, agree with my formulations. I do know, however, that whatever merit the work may have is largely owing to the friendship and generosity they have provided over the years.

Finally, I want to thank Professor Makoto Itoh of the Economics Faculty of Tokyo University, who translated the book into Japanese and contributed a concluding Afterword addressed to Japanese readers. It was in no small part his encouragement which decided me to go ahead with publication of the book at this time despite the fact that, as the reader will see, it contains not a few arguments and conclusions which are put forward in a tentative way and are subject to revision after discussion and further consideration.

—Paul M. Sweezy

New York City
February 1980

INTRODUCTION

As in the case of many people who grew to maturity in the period between the two world wars, my outlook on the world was decisively shaped by two events which simultaneously shook the world in the early 1930s. One was the onset of the Great Depression, the other the launching of the First Five Year Plan in the Soviet Union. Both contradicted the conventional wisdom of the time (not only in the United States, but certainly especially in the United States), and both cried out for explanation. The social science to which I had been exposed in school and college, however, had nothing to offer. In seeking enlightenment, I discovered Marxism. It seemed to have the answers: the depression announced the predicted decline and fall of capitalism, the Five Year Plan the beginning of the new age of socialism which Marxists believed was its necessary and inevitable successor.

What happened in the years that followed seemed to support this interpretation. The rise of Nazism and World War II confirmed capitalism's inability to solve its problems; the emergence from the war of the Soviet Union, intact in spite of enormous losses and sacrifices, proved that the new system was viable, and its spread to vast areas of Eastern Europe and Asia in the years after the war showed that it was indeed a rising historical force.

Of course all was not as plain sailing as this brief summary might seem to suggest. Capitalism, too, survived the war and, under U.S. hegemony, entered a period of vigorous expansion. And Khrushchev's revelations at the Twentieth Congress of the

CPUSSR put Soviet reality in a light very different from that which had long been conveyed by its ideologists and official spokesmen. But this was not the first time in its history that capitalism had enjoyed a period of expansion following a war without changing anything fundamental: the historical timetable was not quite what it had seemed in the period of the Great Depression, but the direction of movement was the same. And a realistic appreciation of the terrible ordeals the Soviet Union had been through made plausible the conclusion that the horrors of the Stalin period were the inevitable price that had to be paid for the survival of the new system. Moreover, the fact that the post-Stalin leadership could tell the truth, or at least a considerable part of it, seemed to bode well for reform and regeneration.

But as time passed doubts began to grow. The worldwide capitalist boom continued with only minor interruptions, and the hoped-for reforms in the Soviet Union hardly went beyond the curbing of the worst and by then clearly counterproductive terrorist methods of Stalin's secret police. Maybe the end of capitalism was not in sight, and maybe the Soviet Union did not prefigure a socialist future.

Looking back, I can see that this was the state of mind in the late 1950s of quite a few of us who had lived through the Great Depression and World War II without losing the vision of a better future in our own lifetimes. It was an unsettling period which seemed to call for a searching reassessment of where we stood and what we believed. But then came another of the cataclysmic events which have been so characteristic of this turbulent century, the Sino-Soviet split. Almost overnight it introduced a whole new set of considerations which changed the shape and dimensions of the problem.

China under the leadership of Mao Tsetung had moved away from the Soviet development model in the late 50s, but the ideological break between the two countries did not surface until 1960 when the Soviet Union abruptly withdrew its technicians from China. This precipitated a lengthy polemical debate which raged in all sections of the international revolutionary movement. The Chinese argued that the Soviet Communists, like the Social Democrats during and after World War II, had abandoned Marxism and had embarked on a course of restoring capitalism internally and of aggressive expansionism internationally. The other side of the coin was that the Chinese Revolution and Mao Tsetung Thought had assumed the historic task of carrying on as the true heirs of classical Marxism. What this meant in terms of revolutionary practice was soon to be revealed with the launching of the Cultural Revolution in 1966, the aims of which were to put politics in command, introduce socialist relations of production along with, rather than subsequent to, the development of the forces of production, and not to lose sight of the long-run communist goal of eliminating the "three great differences" (between mental and manual labor, between industry and agriculture, and between city and country).

To many of us, the Chinese polemic and its practical counterpart came like a breath of fresh air on a hot sultry night. The radical tradition is always in need of renewal, but this was especially true in the aftermath of the failure of what had seemed a promising Soviet reform movement. Clearly something had gone wrong in the Soviet Union, whether or not one accepted the Chinese diagnosis of a capitalist restoration. And with the Chinese moving in a sharply different direction, it seemed equally clear at the time that the Soviet Union did not need to be considered as a prototype of the post-revolutionary society of the twentieth century.

What already before the Sino-Soviet split had seemed a need for a thorough reassessment of many of the ideas commonly accepted by Marxists of my generation now became a matter of urgency for both the theory and practice of the revolutionary movement. How should we view the Soviet Union, now grown to the status of a superpower? Had capitalism really been restored there? If so, when had the process begun and through what stages had it developed? If not, what was the nature of the Soviet system and where was it going? And what about China? Had China, drawing negative lessons from the Soviet experience, finally found the socialist road?

These were of course not totally new questions. But they were posed in a new way, and those of us who had become accustomed to taking it for granted that both the Soviet Union and China were socialist countries, only in different stages of development, could no longer avoid thinking about them in a serious way.

That is what this book is about, a search for answers to these and related questions. It is also a sort of record of how my thinking has evolved in the last decade and a half in response on the one hand to my own perceptions of what has been happening in the societies concerned and on the other hand to attempts by historians and other social scientists to reinterpret their history in the light of present-day realities.

The first chapter, written in collaboration with the late Leo Huberman, was occasioned by the fiftieth anniversary of the October Revolution. It contrasts the actual course of development in the Soviet Union with the claims of the regime's spokesmen and ideologists, stressing the depoliticization of social life and the consequent reliance on familiar bourgeois motivations and incentives to keep the system running. In the light of later developments it seems to me that there was an overestimation of the effectiveness of this system of stimuli in the Soviet context, hence also an exaggeration of the society's stability and capacity for continued quantitative economic growth. These themes recur in later chapters, particularly the last, where the assessment of the Soviet economic potential is much more guarded. The fact that the Soviet Union is a sharply stratified society is emphasized here at the outset, as throughout the book, but no position is as yet taken on whether this implies the emergence of a new ruling class. That comes later: by the end, the contention that there is in fact a new ruling class in the Soviet Union is one of the most important, and doubtless also most controversial, of the book's conclusions. The first chapter proceeds from a consideration of what actually happened in the Soviet Union to ask whether it was inevitable, or whether there were turning points in the country's post-revolutionary history when real choices were open and a different course might have been embarked upon. To some this may seem a futile exercise in historical speculation, but in truth it is much more. If there are no real choices in history, or if we fail to explore those which did exist, how can we ever hope to draw useful lessons from historical experience?

The second chapter considers the events which erupted in Poland in December 1970, arguing that they provide useful insights into the consciousness of workers in a Soviet-bloc country, as well as into the nature of its political system.

The third chapter, originally prepared for delivery to audiences in six Italian cities, presents a Marxist framework for analyzing the problem of the transition to socialism and then seeks to sum up the results of applying this framework to the experiences of the Soviet Union and China, stressing their radical differences but ending with a warning against concluding that China under Mao's leadership was securely on the socialist road. Subsequent events, unfortunately, have shown all too clearly that this warning was well founded.

Chapters 4 and 5 constitute an extended review of the first volume of Charles Bettelheim's monumental work, *Class Struggles in the USSR: First Period, 1917–1923*. The purpose of the review is twofold: to summarize for a nonspecialist readership some of the main themes of what I consider to be an extraordinarily important contribution to the understanding of Soviet history, and to discuss critically some questions of theory and method raised by Bettelheim. In particular I question, without flatly rejecting, the author's espousal of the Chinese thesis that capitalism has been restored in the Soviet Union. Subsequently, this questioning would indeed become a rejection, culminating in the attempt in the final chapter to sketch the main outlines of what I now believe to be a new social formation standing on its own foundation, neither capitalist nor socialist.

Chapter 6 is a summary review of the period of Mao Tsetung's leadership of the Chinese Revolution, singling out for special attention China's rejection of the Soviet development strategy and the meaning of the Maoist doctrine of class struggle in the socialist transitional society. Here again the theme introduced in Chapter 3 of the precariousness of China's hold on the socialist road is stressed, though it was too soon after Mao's death to foresee that his successors, once firmly established in power, would lose no time in abandoning Maoist principles and reverting to the conceptions borrowed from Soviet experience which had guided China's course in the early years after the conquest of state power.

In Chapter 7, I return to Bettelheim's reinterpretation of Soviet history, reviewing the second volume of the work which formed the subject matter of Chapters 4 and 5. Here the focus is on the

1920s, the reasons for and meaning of Stalin's so-called "revolution from above."

Having by this time come to the view that the Soviet Union is a new kind of class society, I felt the need to go back and critically discuss Trotsky's theory of the nature of Soviet society and its updated version as presented by Ernest Mandel, the leading Trotskyist theorist of our day. This task forms the subject matter of Chapter 8, which also contains as a sort of appendix an abbreviated version of my rejoinder to Mandel's reply to the original article.

Chapter 9 is a brief presentation, addressed to a large audience gathered to discuss the nature of Soviet society, of a theme central to the whole book but not made explicit elsewhere, namely, that the failure of actual post-revolutionary societies to confirm the expectation of classical Marxism that socialism would follow capitalism has created a crisis in Marxist theory which is having dire consequences for the international revolutionary movement.

Finally, Chapter 10, based on a talk given to the Faculty of Economics at Tokyo University in November 1979, attempts a reasonably comprehensive, if very brief, presentation of my ideas at that time about the nature of the new class society which exists in the Soviet Union and, in less clear-cut form, in the other post-revolutionary societies that have emerged since World War II. I have been somewhat reluctant to commit these ideas to print, since I am very much aware that they need more criticism and "seasoning." But I am also aware that this book would be seriously incomplete without the last chapter, and I comfort myself with the thought that I am not likely to get the critical discussion needed to move forward unless all these matters are subjected to much more open debate than has been the case to date. If this book helps to promote such debate and discussion, I shall consider it a useful contribution.

1
LESSONS
OF THE SOVIET EXPERIENCE

The October Revolution marked the birth of the historical era of socialism, and for this achievement we celebrate it today as humankind will continue to celebrate it for centuries to come. But there is more to celebrate too. Historically speaking, fifty years are a very short time; and it could easily have happened that during its first half century socialism might have made little headway or might even have been temporarily crushed in its birthplace by the forces of international counterrevolution. That this did not happen, that instead socialism spread in little more than three decades to vast new areas of the earth, is due in very large part to the unprecedentedly rapid industrialization of the Soviet Union in the late 1920s and the 1930s. If this massive industrialization had not been successfully carried through in time, the Soviet Union would have lacked the economic and military strength to withstand the Nazi onslaught of 1941; and the revival of socialism within the USSR and its spread to other lands might not have occurred for many years. Nearly two decades of forced industrialization and total war cost the people of the USSR more than 20 million lives and untold suffering. But these heavy sacrifices were not in vain, nor were those who made them the only beneficiaries. By timely preparation and heroic struggle, the Soviet Union played the decisive role in smashing the fascist bid for world power and thereby kept the road open for the second great advance of socialism in the period after 1945. For these historic achievements no less than for the October Revolution itself, humankind owes a lasting debt of gratitude to the Soviet Union and its people.

Spokesmen for the Soviet regime both at home and abroad claim yet another achievement which they believe humankind should celebrate on this fiftieth anniversary. The Soviet Union, they say, has not only laid the foundations of socialism through nationalizing the means of production, building up industry, and collectivizing agriculture; it has also gone far toward erecting on these foundations the socialist edifice itself—a society such as Marx and Lenin envisaged, still tainted by its bourgeois origins but steadily improving and already well along the road to the ultimate goal of full communism. If this were true, it certainly should be celebrated, perhaps more enthusiastically than any of the other achievements of the first half century of Soviet existence. For then we should know that, at least in principle, humankind has already solved its most fundamental problems and that what is needed now is only time for the Soviet Union to work the solutions out to their ultimate consequences, and determination and will on the part of the rest of the world to follow the Soviet example.

If only it were true! But, alas, apart from the pronouncements of the ideologists and admirers of the Soviet regime, it is extremely difficult to find supporting evidence; while the accumulation of evidence pointing to a quite different conclusion is as persuasive as it is massive.

The facts indicate that relative to most other countries in the world today, the Soviet Union is a stable society with an enormously powerful state apparatus and an economy capable of reasonably rapid growth for the foreseeable future. It is also a stratified society, with a deep chasm between the ruling stratum of political bureaucrats and economic managers on the one side and the mass of working people on the other, and an impressive spectrum of income and status differentials on both sides of the chasm. The society appears to be effectively depoliticized at all levels, hence *a fortiori* nonrevolutionary. In these circumstances the concerns and motivations of individuals and families are naturally focused on private affairs and in particular on individual careers and family consumption levels. Moreover, since the economy is able to provide both an abundance of career openings and a steadily expanding supply of consumer goods, these private motivations are effective in shaping the quantity, quality, allocation, and discipline of the labor force.

But the prevalence of these mechanisms cannot but have a profound influence on the quality of the society and the "human nature" of its members. This is part of the ABC of socialist thought and need not be elaborated upon here: suffice it to say that the privatization of economic life leads necessarily to the privatization of social life and the evisceration of political life. Bourgeois values, bourgeois criteria of success, bourgeois modes of behavior are fostered. Politics becomes a specialty, a branch of the division of labor, like any other career. And of course the other side of the coin is the perpetuation and deepening of that alienation of humans from their fellows and hence from themselves which many socialists have long felt to be the ultimate evil of bourgeois society.

It may be argued that while these tendencies exist—this, we believe, can be denied only by blind apologists—they are not yet dominant and they are being effectively offset by counter-tendencies. In this connection, it is usual to cite the narrowing of the gap in incomes and living standards between the collective-farm peasantry and the urban proletariat, the leveling-up of the lower end of wage and pension scales, the shortening of the working day, and a general rise in living standards. These developments are supposed to be preparing the way for a trans-formation of the social consciousness and morality of the Soviet people. As William Pomeroy explained in an article in the *National Guardian* (July 8, 1967), after an extensive tour around the Soviet Union:

> The Soviet view is that education in communist behavior can go only so far without continually rising living standards. They say they are now "laying the material base for communism," and that the aim is to create the highest living standards in the world and that the "new man" will fully flourish only under conditions of abundance.

What this argument overlooks is that living standards are not only a matter of quantity but also of quality. With negligible exceptions, all Marxists and socialists recognize the necessity of high and rising living standards to the realization of socialist goals and the transition to communism. But this is the beginning of the problem, not the end. It should be obvious by now from the experience of the advanced capitalist countries that higher living standards based on the accumulation of goods for private use— houses, automobiles, appliances, apparel, jewelry, etc.—do not create a "new man"; on the contrary, they tend to bring out the worst in the "old man," stimulating greed and selfishness in the economically more fortunate and envy and hatred in the less fortunate. In these circumstances no amount of "education in communist behavior" can do more than provide a thin disguise for the ugly reality.

But is any other kind of rising living standards, more compatible with the realization of socialist goals, conceivable? The answer is obviously yes. We may concede that a priority charge on a socialist society's increasing production is to provide leaders and more skilled and/or responsible workers with what they need to do their jobs properly. But beyond that, certain principles could be followed: (1) private needs and wants should be satisfied only at a level at which they can be satisfied for all; (2) production of such goods and services should be increased only if and when the increments are large and divisible enough to go around; (3) all other increases in the production of consumer goods should be for collective consumption. As applied to an underdeveloped country, these principles mean that there should be no production of automobiles, household appliances, or other consumer durable goods for private sale and use. The reason is simply that to turn out enough such products to go around would require many years, perhaps even many decades, and if they are distributed privately in the meantime the result can only be to create or aggravate glaring material inequalities. The appropriate socialist policy is therefore to produce these types of goods in forms and quantities best suited to the collective satisfaction of needs: car pools, communal cooking and eating establishments, apartment-house or neighborhood laundries, and so on. Such a policy, it should be emphasized, would mean not only a different *utilization* of goods but also a very different pattern of production. In the case of automobiles in particular, a policy of production for collective needs means a strictly limited production, since for many purposes the automobile is an inefficient and irrational means of transportation. Furthermore, restricting the output of automobiles and concentrating instead on other forms of transportation requires a different pattern of investment in highways, railroads, subways, airports, and so on.

Now, if the Soviet Union had embarked upon a program of raising living standards in this second, socialist, sense there would be every reason to take seriously the contention that, certain appearances to the contrary notwithstanding, they are indeed "laying the material base for communism." But this is certainly not the case; nor could it be the case as long as Soviet society is geared to and dependent upon a system of private incentives.* These matters are all indissolubly tied together. A depoliticized society *must* rely on private incentives; and for private incentives to work effectively, the structure of production *must* be shaped to turn out the goods and services which give the appropriate concrete meaning to money incomes and demands. The only way out of this seemingly closed circle would be a *re*politicization of Soviet society, which would permit a move away from private incentives and hence also a different structure of production and a different composition and distribution of additions to the social product. But repoliticization would also mean much else, including in particular a radical change in the present leadership and its methods of governing—at least a "cultural revolution," if not something even more drastic. This means that short of a major upheaval, which does not seem likely in the foreseeable future, the present course is set for a long time to come. And since, as we have already indicated, this course has little to do with "laying the material base for communism," we have to ask in what direction it is leading.

---

*The debate over incentives is usually couched in terms of "material" vs. "moral." But this is not really accurate, since in both cases material gains are envisaged: the opposition lies rather in the composition of the gains and the way they are distributed. Hence it may be more helpful to speak of "private" vs. "collective" incentives. At the same time it should be recognized that there *is* a moral element in the collective incentive system: behavior directed toward improving the lot of everyone (including oneself) is certainly more moral, and presupposes a higher level of social consciousness, than behavior directed toward immediate private gain.

The answer, we believe, is that it is leading to a hardening of material inequalities in Soviet society. The process by which this is occurring can be seen most clearly in the area of consumer durable goods. For most of Soviet history, the need to concentrate on heavy industry and war production, and to devote most of consumer good production to meeting the elementary requirements of the mass of the population, precluded the possibility of developing industries catering to the latent demand of the higher income strata for consumer durables. In respect to this aspect of the standard of living, which bulks so large in the advanced capitalist countries, there was therefore a sort of enforced equality in the Soviet Union. In the last few years, however, this situation has been changing. Now at last the production of refrigerators, washing machines, automobiles, etc. on an increasing scale has become feasible, and the Soviet government is moving vigorously to develop this sector of the economy. And while a considerable proportion of the output, especially in the case of the automobile industry, will have to be devoted to official and public uses for years to come, nevertheless it is clear that the basic policy is to channel a larger and larger share of consumer durable production into the private market. Some idea of what this portends is conveyed by Harrison Salisbury in an article entitled "A Balance Sheet of Fifty Years of Soviet Rule" in the *New York Times* of October 2, 1967:

> In the fiftieth year of Bolshevik power the Soviet Union stands on the edge of the automobile age that the United States entered in the 1920's. With new production facilities being constructed by Fiat, Renault, and others, the Soviet Union will be turning out 1,500,000 passenger cars a year in the early 1970's, more than five times the present output. But this will not be soon enough to cut off the wave of popular grumbling.
>
> "When I see that any ordinary worker in Italy or France has a car," said a writer just back from one of his frequent trips to Western Europe, "I wonder what we have been doing in the last 50 years. Of course, there has been progress. But it's not fast enough."
>
> The Soviet Union's entry into the automobile age is not going to be easy. The Russian writer owns a car, a 10-year-old Pobeda. He has to keep it on the street all winter in temperatures of 30 below

zero. No garages are available. None are provided in the new apartments or office buildings. Most Moscow car owners drain their radiators every night in winter and fill them in the morning with boiling water to get started. There are three gasoline stations in Moscow selling high-test gasoline. Today there are perhaps 100,000 private cars in Moscow. What will happen when there are a million?

Part of the answer of course is that along with the increase in production of cars, the Soviet Union will have to embark on a vast expansion in the provision of all the facilities required by an automobilized society: highways, garages, service stations, parking lots, motels, and all the rest. And in sum, if American experience is a reliable indicator, these complements to the automobile will absorb an even larger part of the Soviet economy's labor power and material resources than production of the vehicles themselves.

Two points need to be specially emphasized. First, even assuming a continued rapid increase in automobile production, it will be many, many years before more than a small minority of the Soviet population can hope to join the ranks of car owners. During this period, the automobile will add a new dimension to the structure of material inequality in Soviet society, which will by no means be limited to the simple possession of cars. Those who have their own private means of mobility tend to develop a distinctive style of life. The automobile increasingly dominates their use of leisure time (after work, weekends, vacations) and thus indirectly generates a whole new set of needs, ranging from country houses for those who can afford them through camping equipment to all kinds of sporting goods.

Second, and this is a point which is generally neglected but which in our view is of crucial importance, the allocation of vast quantities of human and material resources to the production of private consumer durable goods and their complementary facilities means neglecting or holding back the development of other sectors of the economy and society. Or to put the matter more bluntly: a society which decides to go in for private consumer durables in a big way at the same time decides *not* to make the raising of mass living standards its number one priority.* And these are indeed the decisions which the Soviet leadership has taken and is in the process of vigorously implementing.

To sum up: The course on which the Soviet Union has embarked implies a long period of *increased* material inequality during which productive resources are, directly and indirectly, channeled into satisfying the wants of a privileged minority and mass living standards are raised less rapidly and less fully than would otherwise be possible.

We shall perhaps be told that even if the period in question is of necessity long, it is in principle transitional and will eventually lead, via a process of leveling-up, to a situation in which everyone is a full participant in a society of consumer-durable-goods abundance—or, in other words (since the automobile is by far the dominant consumer durable), to a fully automobilized society. It is a strange conception of socialism, this gadget utopia; but, fortunately or unfortunately, it does not seem very likely to be realized. For if anything is well established on the basis of long and varied historical experience, it is that a ruling stratum which is firmly rooted in power and has accustomed itself to the enjoyment of privileges and emoluments finds ways to preserve and protect its vested interests against mass invasion from below. There already exists such a ruling stratum in the Soviet Union, and the course now being followed guarantees that its privileged position will be enhanced and strengthened for a long time to come. If anyone thinks this stratum is going to renounce its position unless obliged to do so by *force majeure,* he or she is either a dreamer or a believer in miracles. "Laying the material base for communism" seems to be a slogan of the same kind as those even more famous slogans of the eighteenth-century bourgeois revolutions—"life, liberty, and the pursuit of happiness" and "liberté,

---

*With this in mind, we can see how absurd it is to describe the debate between Soviet spokesmen and their critics in the socialist camp as being between those who want the Soviet people to have the "good things of life" and those who would impose on them an artificial austerity. The truth is that it is between those who want a small minority to have the lion's share of the good things and those who think these good things ought to be produced and distributed in forms accessible to the broad masses.

egalité, fraternité"—designed to rally the support of those who look forward to a better future but increasingly divorced from economic and social reality.

The reader will note that we have been careful to speak of a ruling "stratum" rather than a ruling "class." The difference is that the members of a stratum can stem from diverse social origins, while the great majority (though not all) of the members of a class are born into it. A new class usually begins as a stratum and only hardens into a class after several generations during which privileges become increasingly hereditary and barriers are erected to upward mobility. Historically, property systems have been the most common institutional arrangement for ensuring the inheritability of privilege and blocking the upward movement of the unprivileged. But other devices such as caste and hereditary nobility have also served these purposes.

To what extent, if at all, the Soviet system of stratification has developed into a true class system we do not pretend to know. Fifty years—about two generations by usual calculations—is in any case too short a time for the crystalization of such a profound social change. At the present time, therefore, one can only say that conditions favoring the development of a class system exist and that in the absence of effective counter-forces, we must assume that these conditions will bear their natural fruit. And by effective counter-forces we do not mean ideological doctrines or statements of good intentions but organized political struggle. Unless or until signs of such struggle appear, one can only conclude that Soviet stratification will in due course be transformed into a new class system.

That all this is a far cry from the Marxian vision of the future (even the relatively near-term post-revolutionary future) as expressed for example in Marx's *Critique of the Gotha Program* or Lenin's *State and Revolution*, needs no demonstration. This divergence between theory and practice will naturally be interpreted by bourgeois critics as (yet another) proof of the failure of Marxism and as (further) evidence that "you can't change human nature." What is the Marxian answer to these critics? Did it have to happen that way in the Soviet Union? Or might events have taken a different course? These are by no means mere "academic" questions (i.e., questions the answers to which have no practical significance). If what has happened in the Soviet Union had to happen, the chances that other socialist countries, present and future, will be able to escape the same fate would, at the very least, have to be rated low. If on the other hand events might have taken a different course in the Soviet Union, then other socialist countries, learning from Soviet experience, can still hope to prove that Marx and Lenin were right after all and that in entering the era of socialism humankind has at last found the key to a new and qualitatively better future.

What is at issue here is really the age-old question of historical determinism. The determinist position holds essentially that the conditions which exist at any given time uniquely determine what will happen next. This does not necessarily mean that every individual's thoughts and actions are uniquely determined, but only that in the given circumstances only one combination of thoughts and actions can be effectively put into practice. Individuals can choose but societies cannot. At the other extreme, what is often called the voluntarist position holds that anything can happen depending on the will and determination of key individuals or groups.

Marxism is neither determinist nor voluntarist; or, if you prefer, it is both determinist and voluntarist. "Men make their own history," wrote Marx in the second paragraph of *The Eighteenth Brumaire of Louis Bonaparte,* "but they do not make it just as they please; they do not make it under circumstances chosen by themselves, but under circumstances directly encountered, given and transmitted from the past." In other words, at any given time the range of possibilities is determined by what has gone before (determinism), but within this range genuine choices are possible (voluntarism). This very general principle, however, by no means exhausts the Marxian position. Even more important from our present point of view is the idea, which is of the very essence of Marxism as a revolutionary doctrine, that in the life of societies there are long periods of relative stability during which a given social order unfolds and finally reaches the end of its potentialities, and that these are followed by periods of revolutionary transition to a new social order. This theme is of course familiar to all students of Marxism, especially from the famous preface to the *Critique of Political Economy*. What does not seem to have been widely recognized is the clear implication that the ratio of determinism to voluntarism in historical explanation necessarily varies greatly from one period to another. Once a social order is firmly established and its "law of motion" is in full operation, power naturally gravitates into the hands of those who understand the system's requirements and are willing and able to act as its agents and beneficiaries. In these circumstances, there is little that individuals or groups can do to change the course of history: for the time being a strictly determinist doctrine seems to be fully vindicated. But when the inherent contradictions of the system have had time to mature and the objective conditions for a revolutionary transformation have come into existence, then the situation changes radically. The system's law of motion breaks down wholly or in part, class struggles grow in intensity, and crises multiply. Under these circumstances the range of possibilities widens, and groups (especially, in our time, disciplined political parties) and great leaders come into their own as actors on the stage of history. Determinism recedes into the background and voluntarism seems to take over.

If we apply this dialectic of determinism and voluntarism to the interpretation of Soviet history, two conclusions stand out very clearly: First, the early years—from 1917 until the late 1920s, when the country had irrevocably committed itself to forced industrialization and collectivization of agriculture—were a "voluntarist" period during which the Bolshevik Party and its leaders, meaning primarily Lenin and Stalin, played a crucial role in shaping the course of events. There were of course definite limits to what could have been done after the Bolsheviks came to power, but they were wide enough to encompass the course which was actually followed under Stalin at one extreme, and at the other extreme a course (certainly feasible and actually advocated by Bukharin and others in the Bolshevik leadership) of "socialist *laissez faire*" which would have involved surrender to the kulak-dominated market economy and most likely a relatively rapid restoration of capitalism.

The second conclusion which stands out is that in recent

years—at least since the Twentieth Party Congress and the beginning of de-Stalinization—the Soviet Union has entered a "determinist" period in which the party and its leaders are hardly more than cogs in a great machine which is running, sometimes smoothly and sometimes bumpily, along a more or less clearly prescribed course, some of the main aspects of which have been analyzed above.

Now it is clear that the kind of machine which came into being to dominate the "determinist" period was formed in the "voluntarist" period by the conscious decisions and acts of the party leadership, for the most part after Stalin took over. This is not to imply that Stalin had a blueprint of the kind of society he wanted to create and shaped his policies accordingly, though considerations of this kind may have played some role. Between 1928 and the end of World War II, which was certainly the crucial formative period of present-day Soviet society, Stalin was probably mainly motivated by fear of external attack and a supposed need, in the face of this danger, to crush all actual or potential internal opposition. In other words, the kind of society being created in the Soviet Union during these years was in a real sense a by-product of policies designed to accomplish other ends. But, from our present point of view, this is not the important point. What is crucial is that these policies were deliberately decided upon and in no sense a mere reflex of an objective situation. They could have been different. The goal they were intended to achieve could have been different, and the combination of means designed to achieve the goal actually chosen or another goal or set of goals could also have been different. And the result today could have been a different society operating with a different internal logic and following a different course of development.

These are not mere armchair speculations. We *know* that different courses were possible in the decisive years after Lenin's death because we know that great struggles and debates racked the Bolshevik Party in that period. Nothing requires us to believe that Stalin's victory was inevitable, or that if the left or right opposition had won out it would necessarily have followed the same course he followed. The options were real, and the Soviet Union is what it is today because some were embraced and others rejected.

This is not the occasion for a review of the arguments over what policies might have been adopted and their probable consequences: that would be an ambitious undertaking indeed. Suffice it to say that our own view is that Stalin was certainly right to make preparations to repel external aggression the number one priority, but that a different choice of means could have produced better results in the short run and much better results in the long run. More equality and fewer privileges to the bureaucracy, more trust and confidence in the masses, greater inner party democracy—these, we believe, could have been the guiding principles of a course which would have ensured the survival of the Soviet Union and pointed it toward, rather than away from, the luminous vision of a communist future.

Fifty years of Soviet history have many lessons to teach. And of these the greatest and most important, we believe, is that revolutionary societies can and must choose and that how they choose will unavoidably have fateful consequences for many years and decades to come.

(November 1967)

2
LESSONS
OF POLAND

Recent events in Poland cast a revealing light on the situation in that country as it developed under the Gomulka regime, and at the same time raise important questions about the future not only of Poland but also of the other European socialist countries.*

The troubles began with the abrupt announcement on December 13, 1970, of a far-reaching revision of the system of consumer prices. Prices of necessities—food, fuel, and clothing—were increased, in some cases sharply; while prices of durable consumer goods—tape recorders, radios, TV sets, washing machines, refrigerators, vacuum cleaners, etc.—were reduced, generally by 15 percent or more. "In general," wrote James Feron from Warsaw, "the idea was to ease some agricultural shortages [by reducing demand] while shifting consumer spending to industrial goods."[2]

This reform of the price system both highlights one of the great advantages of the socialist system of economic planning, and at the same time demonstrates how badly this system can be abused under the control of an irresponsible bureaucracy.

The advantage in question derives from the fact that in a socialist economic system prices are not (or at any rate need not

---

*The term "socialist" is used here and in what follows (except where the context clearly indicates otherwise) in the sense explained by Isaac Deutscher: "We all speak . . . colloquially about the USSR, China, and the associated and disassociated states as 'socialist countries,' and we are entitled to do so as long as we intend merely to oppose their regimes to the capitalist states, to indicate their post-capitalist character, or to refer to the socialist origins and intentions of their governments and policies."[1]

be) set to maximize the profits of individual enterprises. Under monopoly capitalism, which is the only kind of capitalism in existence today, prices *are* set to maximize profits regardless of the consequences for the system as a whole; and this, together with capitalism's limitless drive to expand, is what accounts for the horrors and irrationalities to which the system inevitably gives rise. Under socialism, on the other hand, prices can be deliberately managed in the general interest and to promote the smooth working of the economy as a whole. In these circumstances, price policy becomes a powerful and invaluable tool of economic planning. "It is indeed paradoxical," wrote the late Michal Kalecki, Poland's greatest economist, "that, while the apologists of capitalism usually consider the 'price mechanism' to be the great advantage of the capitalist system, price flexibility proves to be a characteristic feature of the socialist economy."[3] This has once again been demonstrated by the latest events in Poland.

Powerful tools, however, can be dangerous as well as useful, and this has also been demonstrated by what happened in Poland in December. Poland is run by the Communist Party, which proclaims itself to be a party of the working class dedicated to strengthening socialism and building communism. And yet it is crystal clear that a price reform which raises the prices of necessities and lowers the prices of conveniences and what can even be considered luxuries in a poor country like Poland, that such a price reform imposes the greatest sacrifices on workers and other low-income groups (e.g., those who are too old or too young to work) in the cities, and adds to the already privileged position of urban bureaucrats, professionals, intellectuals, etc. Perhaps the main beneficiaries are the farmers who grow much of their own food and will now be able to expand their purchases of durable consumer goods. If it were within the power of a capitalist government to impose such a price reform (which of course it isn't), a law to carry it out would immediately and rightly be denounced as the grossest form of class legislation. Does the fact that Poland calls itself socialist and is ruled by a Communist Party make it any less so?

No wonder the whole affair was prepared in secret and announced as an accomplished fact without in any way consulting the people most directly affected. The Gomulka regime was obviously hoping to be able to put over a fast one and get away with it. The fact that it badly miscalculated was a reflection of its own isolation from the masses and an indicator of the profound need for political change in Poland. But before we come to that, it is worth noting that the underlying policy expressed in the price reform—imposing the greatest sacrifices on the workers—is quite consistent with the course which not only Poland but at least two of the other Eastern European countries (Czechoslovakia and the German Democratic Republic) have pursued since World War II. In his authoritative study of industrialization in these countries, Alfred Zauberman found that the brunt of forced saving—in other words, socialist accumulation—was borne by the industrial workers rather than by the peasantry (as had been the case at a comparable stage of development in the USSR).[4] This was pointed out to us by Lynn Turgeon, who spent several months in 1970 studying the same area at first hand. Turgeon concluded that the farmers have been among the chief beneficiaries of the new system in northeastern Europe, and that their economic position there is somewhat analogous to that of capitalist farmers in a wartime seller's market. He was particularly impressed with a great improvement in rural housing that he observed all over the region.

The announcement of the price reform triggered large-scale demonstrations in the Baltic port cities, especially Gdansk, Gdynia and Szczecin (most likely in cities in other parts of the country as well, but the fewness of foreign correspondents and censorship of local means of communication have so far kept outsiders, and probably most Poles too, in the dark about what happened in the country as a whole). The first reaction of the regime was exactly what one would expect from leaders brought up in the orthodox Communist tradition. The logic is all too familiar: the party represents the interests of the working class, hence anyone criticizing or opposing party policies must be an enemy of the working class. Accordingly, blame for the demonstrations was automatically attributed to hooligans, troublemakers, criminal elements, etc.; and the forces of repression (police and army) were turned loose on the demonstrators. Estimates of casualties vary widely, but they were certainly counted in the scores and maybe in the hundreds (according to one Swedish account, reported in the *New York Times*, the death toll in Gdansk alone was three hundred).

A very different picture of what happened emerges from the reports of newsmen who either were themselves eyewitnesses or were able to interview those who were. And what confirms the general accuracy of these reports is that after Gomulka's ouster (to which we shall return presently), the government itself began to sing an entirely different tune. The actual course of events seems to have been somewhat as follows: The trouble began with shipyard workers who held meetings in their places of work and then proceeded to Communist Party headquarters with what we may surmise were mixed motives—some to demand explanations, some to protest, some to vent long-pent-up anger. Being met with repression rather than attempts at explanation, they attacked and in some cases destroyed party buildings, police stations, and other symbols of authority. Large crowds were involved—one report from Szczecin estimates 10,000 people—and the army was called in to restore order. The same report from Szczecin tells of factories being occupied for several days "until a truce was arranged: a return to work against the removal of the tanks and a promise of no reprisals against the workers."[5]

Back in Stalin's time a Communist government confronted with such a situation would have reacted with mass arrests, show trials, executions, imprisonments, and deportations to labor camps. The status quo ante would have been brutally restored and enforced. But Poland left that period at least as long ago as 1956, the year of Khrushchev's famous attack on Stalin and of the first wave of liberalization in the Eastern European satellite countries. That was also the year of the Poznan riot in Poland, an occurrence which bore a striking resemblance, only on a smaller scale, to the events of this last December. In both cases the triggering factor was economic discontent; in both cases the government in power began by laying the blame on hostile elements; and in both cases this explanation was soon dropped. A recent writer on the earlier period, noting that at the time of the Poznan riot the official line was that it was an imperialist plot, proceeded as follows:

> But after a few days of reflection . . . Ochab [then head of the party]
> admitted that riots were *not* an imperialist plot and that recently
> published figures claiming to show how the standard of living had
> risen were imaginary. From then on the official Polish line was that
> the rioters were largely justified in taking the action they did. Later
> he even had the humility to lay part of the blame on himself and his
> comrades: "It is a fact that our leadership was unable to protect the
> country from the tragedy of Poznan, that we were all astounded
> when the tragedy took place. This means that our awareness of the
> actual situation, of actual moods in the country, was insufficient
> and superficial."[6]

In one respect, however, and despite many statements to the
contrary in the media during the last few weeks, what happened
in 1970 did not resemble what happened in 1956. The Poznan
riot did not result in a change in party leadership or government.
It makes a nice journalistic story to say that Gomulka went out the
same way he came in, in the wake of working-class demonstrations. But it isn't true. The Poznan riot took place on June 28,
1956, and Gomulka returned to power, after nearly a decade in
the political wilderness, on October 19, nearly four months later.
Further, as is well known, the crisis which brought him back to the
leadership of party and nation was precipitated not by the Poznan
riot but by a threat of Soviet military intervention such as actually
materialized in Hungary two weeks later. Still, what Gomulka had
to say about Poznan in his first major speech after returning to
power is well worth remembering today:

> Recently the working class gave a painful lesson to the Party leader-
> ship and government. The workers of Poznan made use of the
> strike weapon and came out into the street to demonstrate on that
> black Thursday in June, calling out in a loud voice, "Enough! We
> cannot go on like this! Turn aside from the false road!" . . . The
> workers of Poznan were not protesting against People's Poland,
> against socialism, when they came out into their city streets. They
> were protesting against the evil that has become so widespread in
> our social system and which touched them so painfully, against
> distortions of the basic rules of socialism, which is their ideal. . . .
> The clumsy attempt to present the painful Poznan tragedy as the
> work of imperialist agents and *agents provocateurs* was politically
> very naive.[7]

What else do the events of last December show if not that this same Gomulka in his fourteen years of undisputed leadership of the Polish Communist Party either forgot the lessons of Poznan or was unwilling or unable to apply them to the governance of the country? That when the workers once again cried out "Enough! We cannot go on like this!" he showed himself to be no more original or no less naive politically than his predecessors?

Gomulka entered office in 1956 enjoying great popularity and prestige. He left in 1970, just one week after the announcement of the price reform, discredited and unlamented. Divisions within the party leadership had apparently already reached an advanced stage, and Gomulka's once solid support had melted away. Faced with crisis and the evident need to placate the angry workers, the Central Committee acted quickly to dump its long-time chief and to replace him with the man considered most likely to be acceptable to the workers.

That man is Edward Gierek, son of a coal miner and himself originally a miner who lived for many years in France and Belgium (where he served as chairman of the Polish section of the Belgian Communist Party after World War II). Back in Poland he studied for an engineering degree, rose to the top position in the party in the Katowice coal-mining area, and was elected to the Politburo in 1959. According to press reports, Gierek managed to get special treatment for the miners in such matters as housing and distribution of consumer goods and in this way built up a considerable base of working-class support. It was presumably this which made him the party's choice to succeed Gomulka at a time of working-class rebellion.

As always happens in one-party political systems when one leader replaces another, everyone immediately feels freer to criticize the conditions that led up to the change and that can now be blamed on the sins of the deposed. It is therefore in such times that we can expect to get some insight into how things work, even if criticisms are often couched in an indirect way. Take, for example, some of the things Gierek, the new leader, said in his December 20 TV speech on assuming the position of first secretary of the party:

The iron rule of our economic policy and our policy in general must always take reality into account as well as wide-ranging consultation with the working class and intelligentsia, respect for the principle of collective leadership and democracy in the life of the party and in the activity of top authorities.

The recent events remind us in a painful way of this basic truth, that the party must always maintain close links with the working class and the whole nation, that it must not lose a common language with the working people.[8]

One's first reaction to this may be that there is nothing remarkable about it, that it is merely a reiteration of commonplaces that have been current in the socialist movement for generations. And yet, interpreted in context, what Gierek is saying in these few sentences is: (1) that in formulating its policies the goverment had not been in the habit of taking account of reality; (2) that it had neglected to consult the working class and the intelligentsia; (3) that it had ignored the principle of collective leadership and democracy in the life of the party; and (4) that it had failed to maintain close links with the working class and did not speak a common language with the working people. Quite some confessions for a party which defines itself as the vanguard of the proletariat!

Or take the opening sentence of the *New York Times* report on Gierek's New Year's Eve speech to the nation: "Edward Gierek, Poland's new Communist Party leader, pledged today that government policy in 1971 would be honest, direct, clear and understandable to everyone." What else is this but an admission that in the past goverment policy has been dishonest, indirect, and incomprehensible to ordinary people?

Revealing as these confessions and admissions are, however, it is important not to be misled into assuming that they reach to the heart of the problem of what is wrong in Poland today. An analogy with our own situation in the United States may help to clarify matters. No accusation has been more frequently or more justifiably leveled against the U.S. government, especially since the Americanization of the Vietnam war in 1965, than that of lying to the people. This has gone so far now that the term "credibility gap"—meaning the gap between the truth and what the government says—has become a household byword. Richard Nixon, like Lyndon Johnson before him, is continuously and rightly charged, and not only by the left, with hypocrisy, double-dealing, and deceit. But does anyone imagine that all would be well if only the president would tell the truth about what is going on? If instead of claiming to be for self-determination of the people of South Vietnam he came out and stated that it is U.S. policy to maintain a neocolony there? If instead of claiming that he is withdrawing armed forces from Vietnam he admitted that he intends to perpetuate U.S. armed occupation?

No, it is not the lying that is at the bottom of the matter but the policies about which a government feels it necessary to lie. The lying only shows that the government knows its policies are unacceptable to the mass of people and hence wishes to hide the truth. The obverse is that a government can tell the truth, and has every reason to want to tell the truth, only when its policies are really those which the mass of the people accept and want. And a corollary is that a government can know its policies are the ones the people want only if it is the wants of the people which shape these policies—in other words, only if the principle "from the masses to the masses" is scrupulously observed. Taking account of the truism that individuals or groups are always fallible, we can carry the reasoning one step further and say that a government can be relied upon to practice "from the masses to the masses" consistently and persistently only if in the last analysis it is controlled by the masses. The surest test of the existence of genuine democracy in a given country is therefore the truthfulness of its government.

With respect to Poland, two things follow: First, by its leaders' own admission it has been the opposite of a democracy. And second, Gierek's promises to give up the old ways of deceit and obscurantism can be carried out only if his government now embarks on a course honestly respectful of, and responding to, the wants of the Polish masses, the great majority of whom now live in the cities and towns, and most of whom are in or close to the working class.

What do these masses really want? It seems to us that there may be a clue here in the pretty clear evidence that they do *not* want what their rulers have been trying to force down their throats. In this connection, we found extremely illuminating a short piece by Harry Schwartz, the *New York Times*'s expert on the Soviet bloc, which appeared in the paper's Business and Finance section on January 10. The main headline is "East-Bloc Reform," and the subhead is "Efforts to Spur Poland's Workers Backfired." Here is the integral text of Schwartz's article:

A cynical Eastern European slogan, "Communism is Better than Working," may be in for a new lease on life as a result of the Polish disturbances that toppled Wladyslaw Gomulka, the Communist Party leader.

Those disturbances were touched off directly by efforts to reform the Polish economy to provide incentives and prods for greater worker productivity. Mr. Gomulka's fall seems likely to discourage other proponents of economic reform in Eastern Europe and the Soviet Union because it demonstrates the serious political consequences that can result.

The economic reforms introduced in the nineteen-sixties differed considerably from one Communist-ruled nation to another. Nevertheless, all aim at obtaining greater market influence on production, bringing prices and wages closer to what is required by supply and demand conditions, and giving industrial and other executives more flexibility and freedom in making managerial decisions than they had under the detailed central economic planning of the past.

Observers have pointed out that the shipyard workers of Gdansk who began the recent disorders were upset at least as much by proposals to change the complex regulations governing their wages as by the higher prices announced for food, fuel, and other essentials. The workers feared that the wage changes would lower their weekly earnings, while the economic reformers were hoping that precisely this fear would induce the Polish workers to increase their efforts and productivity.

Against this background, some observers point out, it is now clear that hostility to such economic reforms is at least as great in the working class of the Soviet-bloc countries involved as among the economic managers who are used to old ways and are reluctant to try new ones.

In effect, much of Eastern Europe and the Soviet Union has operated under a kind of informal social contract understood and honored by all concerned. This contract provided that everyone would be guaranteed a job and at least a minimum subsistence level so long as he showed up for work and seemed to exert himself. It has been a lazy man's delight, a bargain in which many workers have gladly exchanged minimal effort for minimal, but secure, wages.

In much of Eastern Europe, workers who want to do better economically than their factory wage permitted have usually moonlighted. They have worked hard as independent craftsmen, artisans, or builders on their time off, and some have looked at their time in the factory as a rest period in which they could recuperate from the work that was really profitable.

All this has been possible because of the lack of domestic competition in each Soviet-bloc country and because of the egalitarian bias in much of Eastern Europe. The latter feeling has produced social pressure to discourage any worker from being more energetic than average and from earning more pay than average.

But in the nineteen-seventies, the Eastern European countries and the Soviet Union are having to face up to the fact that they must meet international competition, and their costs of production and the quality of their goods must be improved so they can be sold in world markets against American, German, British, French, Japanese, and other competition. The spur of this competition was emphasized by Polish officials last month when they tried to win public support for economic reform and price increases.

To Eastern European workers, however, talk of international competition and balance-of-payments problems is almost incomprehensible. Instead the workers see the economic reform and the specific measures associated with it as a means of disturbing the comfortable status quo, while they threaten lower wages for a large number of workers who cannot or will not improve their productivity.

Given the wide prevalence of egalitarian feeling in the area, many workers view the incentive features of the reform with great suspicion. Why should some workers earn more than others, they ask. Isn't that a return to the dog-eat-dog competition of capitalism, which socialism was supposed to abolish?

In the Soviet Union, the greatest suspicion among the workers of economic reform has arisen from the fear that it would bring unemployment. It is common knowledge in the Soviet bloc that many factories and mines are overstaffed. Hence one way a factory operating under the economic reform can improve its profits is to dismiss its surplus workers.

Soviet propagandists have tried to reassure workers that dismissal of surplus workers did not mean unemployment because, supposedly, there were many unfilled jobs that the newly dismissed workers could take. But the fear that economic reform can lead to unemployment persists. Many workers are aware that such unfilled jobs are often in distant places, for example in the Siberian oil fields, where they do not want to go.

Eastern European economic managers have been most successful in solving these problems when they have introduced reforms affecting workers slowly, rather than introducing many major changes at one time without warning as occurred when Polish prices rose sharply earlier last month.

The implications of this analysis are far-reaching indeed. Its basic assumption, the reality of which is evident enough to an informed bourgeois observer like Schwartz, is that there exists a profound split between the "economic managers" (i.e., the ruling bureaucracies) on the one hand and the workers on the other. *The managers operate according to what are essentially capitalist standards.* Their economic thinking and decision-making are directed to the goals of production, productivity, competitiveness in international markets: these are seen as ends, not means. And the means to these ends are precisely the workers who are to be manipulated by propaganda, incentive schemes, fear of loss of income, dread of unemployment, etc. This not only *resembles* the economic ideology of capitalism, it *is* the economic ideology of capitalism.

The workers react in classical proletarian fashion. Looking upon work as a part of living and not simply as a way to make money, they resent being subjected to all the typical capitalist tricks to make them work harder. They suffer from an "egalitarian bias" and do not want to be pitted against each other in a dog-eat-dog scramble. They prefer a secure lower income to an insecure higher one. They do not want to be uprooted from their familiar environment and human associations to be sent hither and yon in accordance with the dictates of some far-away bureaucrat. They are, in short, proletarians and not upward-striving individualists. The old centrally planned socialist regimes, for all their shortcomings, did give them some of the things they value. They do not propose to give these things up in exchange for a promise of more GNP or foreign currency reserves or any other abstraction which happens to dominate the calculations of economic planners and party functionaries.

This does not at all mean that East European workers are, as Schwartz seems to imply, lazy, hopelessly conservative, opposed to all progress, etc. What it does mean is that they are not good material on which to build a modernized state capitalist system fit to compete for international markets against advanced monopoly capitalist countries like West Germany, the United States, and Japan. In other words, East European workers have not been imbued with capitalist values and motivations, and they are not in the least interested in helping their upstart bosses to get into the capitalist big league. Given a choice between a "comfortable status quo" and working their heads off for something they find incomprehensible, they unhesitatingly choose the former.

But suppose they were offered a different alternative, the alternative of actively participating in the planning and building of a better society in a sense they *can* comprehend—a society with higher incomes not for some but for all, with more not less security, with expanded opportunities for developing and deepening the human associations they so obviously cherish, with increasing power to control the conditions of their work and the quality of their lives. To put the point in another way, suppose their leaders, instead of slavishly following in the footsteps of the capitalists, were to boldly "put politics in command" and proclaim the goal of a truly proletarian socialist society. Who dares to predict that, given *this* choice, the response of the workers would be rejection and noncooperation?

The Harry Schwartzes of course will dismiss this as a pipe dream. They say, with no doubts or qualifications, that "in the 1970's, the Eastern European countries and the Soviet Union are *having* to face up to the *fact* that they *must* meet international competition, that their costs of production and the quality of their goods *must* be improved so they can be sold in world markets against American, German, British, French, Japanese and other competition" (from above-quoted article, emphasis added). To this the answer is, flatly and categorically: nonsense. There is no law of nature or economics that says the Eastern European countries and the Soviet Union have to get into a rat race with the capitalist world. They have the necessary resources, technology, and scientists to choose their own course and to proceed at their own pace. This of course would require the exclusion of techologically more advanced capitalist enterprises from direct participation in their economies, but it would not mean foregoing trade with the capitalist world insofar as such trade might be advantageous for socialist development. As the Soviet economist Evgeny Preobrazhensky wrote nearly half a century ago: "The pressure of capitalist monopolism can be resisted only by socialist monopolism."[9] Anyone who doubts the feasibility of this alternative should look to China, which has already embarked on a course of socialist development independent of, but not cut off from, the capitalist world. And as John Gurley shows in a remarkable article, China, far from collapsing into ignominious failure, has set an example to the world which cannot but have a profound and growing influence as time goes by.[10]

But saying that the objective possibility and probably also the mass base for a turn to socialism exists in the Soviet bloc is altogether different from saying that such a development is at all likely in the near future. As the example of Poland illustrates, the bureaucratic regimes in power in that part of the world are not only separated from the working class, they are profoundly opposed to it in the same sense that the bourgeoisie is opposed to the working class in the capitalist countries. During the week of December 13–20, the Polish workers toppled a government leadership, but they did not topple a regime. Faces have changed, and the new government has been forced to make concessions to popular demands the extent and importance of which remain to be seen.[11] But there is no indication of any fundamental change. The harshness and arbitrariness of bureaucratic rule may be mitigated, but it remains bureaucratic rule. And even modest hopes for a Polish New Deal must be tempered by recollection of the Gomulka experience. The euphoria of 1956 did not last long, and in the later years of his rule Gomulka, the nationalist and reformer, turned into an eager tool of Soviet hegemony and a tyrant to his own people.

The best that could come of the Polish upheaval of 1970 would be if the workers not only of Poland but of the whole Soviet bloc would draw the lesson that what they need is not a new leadership which *claims* to represent their interests but a new regime which *does in fact* represent their interests because it is under their own control.

(February 1971)

3
TRANSITION
TO SOCIALISM

The subject of this talk is so large and one hour is so brief that I must confine myself to a few aspects of what could easily constitute the content of an entire course of lectures. This necessarily means that I will assume much that is neither obvious nor uncontroversial. It may therefore be useful at the outset to make explicit some of these assumptions.

(1) There is no such thing as a general theory of the transition between social systems. This is not because relatively little attention has been paid to the subject—though this is undoubtedly true—but because each transition is a unique historical process which must be analyzed and explained as such.

(2) Nevertheless, a comparative study of transitions can be extremely valuable. In particular the study of past transitions can help us to ask fruitful questions about present and possible future transitions, to recognize similarities and differences, to appreciate the historicity and totality of the process under examination.

(3) Transitions are never simple or brief processes. On the contrary, they typically occupy and even define whole historical epochs. One aspect of their complexity is what may be called multi-directionality: movement in one direction may turn back on itself and resume in a forward direction from a new basis. In some places the reversal may be prolonged or conceivably even permanent.

(4) Transitions from one social order to another involve the most difficult and profound problems of historical materialism. "Herr Proudhon does not know," Marx wrote in *The Poverty of*

Philosophy, "that all history is but the continuous transformation of human nature."[1] This view can be squared with the principle, as stated in the sixth thesis on Feuerbach, that the "human essence is no abstraction inherent in each single individual" but the "ensemble of social relations," only if it is possible to relate the transformation of human nature to the transformation of social relations. How this is to be done is also indicated in the *Theses on Feuerbach* (the third):

> The materialist doctrine that men are products of circumstances and upbringing, and that therefore changed men are the product of other circumstances and changed upbringing, forgets that it is men who change circumstances and that the educator must himself be educated. . . . The coincidence of the changing of circumstances and human activity can be conceived and rationally understood only as *revolutionizing practice*.

Here, in the concatenation of human nature, social relations, and revolutionizing practice, we reach the heart of the problem of the transition from one social system to another.

I would like now to attempt to draw some of the implications of this view for the transition to socialism. Bourgeois human nature was formed in a centuries-long process of actual capitalist development within the framework of feudal society. When capitalism had grown strong enough to challenge and defeat feudalism, there was no real possibility of a return to feudalism. Bourgeois humans were at home only in bourgeois society: there was no conceivable reason for them to reactivate or recreate feudal social relations. (This is not to deny of course that capitalist power could here and there be defeated by feudal power, resulting in local and perhaps even prolonged setbacks to the progress of capitalism. Such occurrences, however, could not arrest the general advance of the new system.) It is altogether different in the case of the transition to socialism. Socialist human nature is not formed within the framework of capitalism but only in the struggle *against* capitalism. What guarantee is there that this will occur on a sufficient scale and in sufficient depth to make possible the construction of a new socialist society? For we should be under no illusion that the social relations specific to a socialist society could exist in anything but name in the absence of the kind of human material which alone could give them sense and meaning. That Marx himself understood this, even if he did not explore all its implications, is shown by a passage from the *Enthüllungen über den Kommunisten-Prozess zu Köln* in which he distinguishes between the propaganda of his group in the Communist League and that of an opposed minority group:

> While we say to the workers: you have to undergo fifteen, twenty, fifty years of civil wars and popular struggles not only to change the relations but to change yourselves and prepare yourselves for political mastery, they tell them on the contrary, "We must come to power immediately, or we can forget about it." While we make a special point of emphasizing to the German worker the underdeveloped state of the German proletariat, they flatter his national feeling and the craft prejudice of the German artisan, which to be sure is more popular.[2]

Here Marx puts his finger on the central issue: the proletariat must not only change the relations of society but in the process change itself. And unfortunately more than a century of subsequent history proves all too conclusively that there is as yet no guarantee that this can be successfully accomplished.

As far as the industrially advanced countries are concerned, capitalism proved to have a great deal more expansive and adaptive power than Marx suspected. Under the circumstances, their proletariats succumbed to economism, which Lenin saw as natural to them but believed could be overcome by a conscious revolutionary vanguard. What actually happened was the opposite: the vanguards, whether calling themselves socialist or social democratic or communist, instead of converting the proletarian masses to revolutionary socialism were themselves transformed into economistic reformers. There are of course those who see in this a temporary aberration and believe that a new revolutionary period has opened in which the proletariat will once again play the role attributed to it in classical Marxist-Leninist theory. I for one fervently hope that they are right, but for now the most one can say is that the case is unproved.

When we turn to the countries where the old regimes (either capitalist or a feudal-capitalist mixture) have actually been overthrown, we are confronted with two very different experiences which, for obvious reasons, can best be exemplified by the Soviet Union and China respectively.

The October Revolution proved the validity, under conditions existing in Russia in 1917, of the first half of the Marxist-Leninist theory of transition to socialism. The industrial proletariat, though relatively small, was able, under resolute revolutionary leadership, to overthrow the bourgeois regime which had come to power in the February Revolution. But with regard to the second half of the theory—the capacity of the proletariat to lead the way in the construction of socialism—the Russian experience is at best inconclusive. Small to begin with, the Russian proletariat was decimated and dispersed by the four years of bloody civil war, hunger, and chaos which followed the October Revolution. The Bolshevik government, preoccupied with problems of survival and economic recovery, was obliged to rely on the old, obviously profoundly antisocialist state bureaucracy and to add to its size and power in the ensuing years. Nevertheless, the period from roughly 1922 to 1928 was one of revolutionary ferment—in the arts, education, sexual relations, social science, etc.—which, had it not been cut short, might have generated powerful socialist forces and trends. What brought this period to an end was the fateful decision to subordinate everything else to the most rapid possible economic development. It would take us too far afield to discuss the reasons for or justification of this decision: suffice it to point out that it entailed what may almost be called a cultural counter-revolution, together with the imposition of an extremely repressive political regime. Under the circumstances, revolutionizing practice tending to produce socialist human nature almost totally disappeared. Instead, the reconstituted and expanded proletariat which came with forced-march industrialization was repressed and atomized, deprived of all means of self-expression, and terrorized by an omnipresent secret police.

While the Russian experience thus throws little light on the positive side of the problem of constructing socialism, it does provide devastating proof of the impossibility of infusing seemingly socialist forms—such as nationalized means of production and comprehensive economic planning—with genuine socialist content unless the process goes hand-in-hand with the formation of socialist human beings. The idea, assiduously promoted by Soviet ideologists, that raising the material living standards of the masses will by itself foster socialist consciousness never had anything to recommend it and has been shown by Soviet (as well as American!) experience to be nonsense. Some of the negative potentialities of the Soviet system were, paradoxically, held in check for a time by the Stalinist terror: a bureaucrat abusing his position too blatantly was likely to find himself in a labor camp, if not worse. But after Stalin's death these restraints were largely removed, and the true nature of the situation was soon revealed.

A recent Chinese critique points to the heart of the matter:

> From production to distribution, from economic branches to government organizations, the forces of capitalism run wild in town and countryside. Speculation, cornering the market, price rigging, and cheating are the order of the day: capitalist roaders in enterprises and government team up in grafting, embezzling, working for their own benefit at the expense of the public interest, dividing up the spoils and taking bribes. Socialist ownership by the whole people has degenerated into ownership by a privileged stratum, and is directly manipulated by a handful of capitalist roaders and new bourgeois elements. . . . This has been a painful historical lesson![3]

I would stress particularly the statement that "socialist ownership by the whole people has degenerated into ownership by a privileged stratum" with the caveat that this is to be interpreted *de facto* rather than *de jure*. It is a privileged stratum—what Charles Bettelheim has called a new "state bourgeoisie"—which controls the means of production and thereby decides how the fruits of production are to be utilized. Regardless of legal forms, this is the real content of class ownership.

It is noteworthy that the foregoing characterization of the situation in the Soviet Union could be applied with little or no change to almost any capitalist country, the main difference being that under capitalism a large part of the activities alluded to are perfectly legal. This underscores the fact that no legal system, using the term in the broadest sense to include the system of property relations, can effectively control people's behavior unless it is in harmony with the historically formed human nature of its subjects. This condition is patently not fulfilled in the Soviet Union.

This of course does not mean that there will never be socialism in the Soviet Union, still less that the failure of the first effort to introduce it has been without positive effects. The earliest appearances of capitalism were also abortive, but they left a precious heritage of experience (including, for example, the invention of double-entry bookkeeping) without which later capitalisms might also have failed or at any rate found development much more difficult. It was through the Russian Revolution that the crucially important science of Marxism-Leninism reached the peoples of Asia, Africa, and Latin America; and it is probably no exaggeration to say that it was only the negative example of later Soviet experience which enabled other countries to see the necessity of protracted revolutionizing practice to the building of socialism. "The restoration of capitalism in the Soviet Union and certain other socialist countries," said Lin Piao on the fiftieth anniversary of the October Revolution, "is the most important lesson to be drawn from the last fifty years of the history of the international communist movement."[4]

It was not, however, only the negative lesson of the Soviet experience which impelled the Chinese to pioneer a different road to the construction of socialism. The situation in China differed in important respects from that in Russia. For one thing, the Chinese proletariat, though smaller than the Russian, was never seriously plagued by economism. As Mao wrote in 1939, "Since there is no economic basis for economic reformism in colonial and semi-colonial China as there is in Europe, the whole proletariat, with the exception of a few scabs, is most revolutionary."[5] To this consistently revolutionary force there was added another even larger one formed in the quarter century of military struggle against capitalism, feudalism, and imperialism, which culminated in the triumph of the revolution in 1949. In the words of the editors of *Hongqi:*

> Owing to the education and training received in the people's army, millions of ordinary workers and peasants and many students and other intellectuals of petty-bourgeois origin have gradually revolutionized themselves [in thinking and action] and become

steadfast, politically conscious fighters and mainstays in revolution and construction.[6]

The prolonged civil war in China, combined with the war against the Japanese invaders, thus fostered a vast growth in both the size and the maturity of the revolutionary forces, while a much shorter period of civil war and resistance to foreign invaders in the Soviet Union seriously weakened the revolutionary forces there. The result was that China, on the morrow of the revolution, was much more richly endowed with revolutionary human material than Russia had been. Finally, in Lenin and Mao Tsetung Russia and China were fortunate to have two of the greatest revolutionary geniuses of all time; but Lenin died before the process of constructing socialism had really begun, while Mao's leadership has already lasted more than two decades since the victory of the revolution.

Both men were well aware of the enormous difficulty of the task that lay ahead after the overthrow of the old regime. In his "Report at the Second All-Russia Trade Union Congress" (January 10, 1919), Lenin said:

> The workers were never separated by a Great Wall of China from the old society. And they have preserved a good deal of the traditional mentality of capitalist society. The workers are building a new society without themselves having become new people, or cleansed of the filth of the old world; they are still standing up to their knees in that filth. We can only dream of cleaning the filth away. It would be utterly utopian to think this could be done all at once. It would be so utopian that in practice it would only postpone socialism to kingdom come.
>
> No, that is not the way we intend to build socialism. We are building while still standing on the soil of capitalist society, combating all those weaknesses and shortcomings which also affect the working people and which tend to drag the proletariat down. There are many old separatist habits and customs of the small holder in this struggle, and we still feel the effects of the old maxim: "Every man for himself, and the devil take the hindmost."[7]

Mao was even more explicit when he wrote, as the People's Liberation Army was about to win its final victories in March 1949:

> To win country-wide victory is only the first step in a long march

of ten thousand *li*. Even if this step is worthy of pride, it is comparatively tiny; what will be more worthy of pride is yet to come. After several decades, the victory of the Chinese people's democratic revolution, viewed in retrospect, will seem like only a brief prologue in a long drama. A drama begins with a prologue, but the prologue is not the climax. The Chinese revolution is great, but the road after the revolution will be longer, the work greater and more arduous.[8]

After only two decades we can see how right Mao was. The drama has continued to unfold, moving from one climax to another. Despite all its initial advantages, China has never been free of the danger of slipping back into the old forms and relations which for centuries had molded Chinese human nature. The old "ensemble of social relations" continued and still continues to exist in the minds and consciousness of hundreds of millions of Chinese. As Marx expressed it in *The Eighteenth Brumaire,* "The tradition of all the dead generations weighs like a nightmare on the brain of the living." To overcome this ineluctable fact—not to nationalize property or build heavy industry or raise material living standards, important though all these things are— is the central problem of the transition to socialism. And it was the Chinese revolutionaries under the inspired leadership of Mao Tsetung who grasped and internalized this truth to the extent of making it the conscious basis of their revolutionizing practice.

This is not the occasion for an attempt to analyze this revolutionizing practice, nor do I have the knowledge and competence which would be required. What I wish to emphasize is that *for the first time* the problem has been fully recognized and correctly posed. Until that was done, there was not even a chance of finding a satisfactory solution.

It is as well to close on a note of caution. In politics, as in science, the first step in solving a problem is to recognize and pose it correctly. But the first step is usually a long way from the final solution, and when the problem is nothing less than changing human nature this *caveat* is doubly and triply relevant. Fortunately, Mao knows this better than anyone else, and we can hope that the knowledge will become a permanent part of his legacy to the Chinese people. Ultimate success or failure will probably not be known until all of us are long since gone and forgotten. As Mao said in 1967, at the height of the Cultural Revolution:

> The present Great Proletarian Cultural Revolution is only the first of its kind. In the future such revolutions must take place. . . . All party members and the population at large must guard against believing . . . that everything will be fine after one, two, three, or four cultural revolutions. We must pay close attention, and we must not relax our vigilance.[9]

All history, Marx said, is the continuous transformation of human nature. What is Mao telling us but that even after the overthrow of class domination the positive task of transforming human nature never ceases?

(Spring 1971)

4
THE NATURE
OF SOVIET SOCIETY—
PART 1

Charles Bettelheim's new book, *Class Struggles in the USSR: First Period, 1917–1923,* is the first volume of what promises to be a work of enormous importance for the world revolutionary socialist movement.[1] Further volumes, dealing respectively with the period 1923–1930 and the years since, are to follow. In this and the next chapter, I propose to do three things: (1) summarize parts of the author's forty-page foreword, in which he relates how the work came to be undertaken and what its purpose is; (2) indicate some of the major themes analyzed for the years 1917–1923 (from the October Revolution to Lenin's death); and (3) raise some questions of theory and method.

Bettelheim's project

The immediate point of departure for *Class Struggles* was the Soviet invasion of Czechoslovakia. Those who consider themselves Marxists, Bettelheim argues, cannot be content to "condemn" or "regret" political acts: it is also necessary to explain them. Regrets and wishes may help people to support their ills, but they do not help to overcome them. On the other hand, by revealing the reasons for what is bad, from the point of view of the interest of the workers, one may contribute to the development of political forces which can prevent regrettable occurrences from happening again in the future. In the case of the invasion of

Czechoslovakia, Bettelheim deemed it all the more necessary not
to limit himself to regrets, since what is at stake is nothing less than
what the Soviet Union has become today.

Bettelheim next gives us the background of his interest in the
problems of the Soviet Union, beginning in 1934 when he began
to learn Russian, and extending through forty years of study, in
the course of which he wrote a considerable number of books on
the Soviet system, on the theory of planning, and on the transition
to socialism. I would like to quote here in full a passage which
sums up not only Bettelheim's original approach to these problems, but also my own and, I am sure, that of innumerable other
Marxist socialists of our generation:

> Basically, my interest in the Soviet Union since the mid-1930s has
> been determined by identification of what was happening in that
> country with the first experience of socialist construction. Without
> being blind to the difficulties and contradictions that marked this
> process (how could I be, when I was in Moscow in 1936, at the time
> of the first of the "great trials," and was able to sense every day the
> confusion into which the city's inhabitants had been thrown and the
> fear of voicing their opinions that was felt by the most ordinary
> people as well as by old members of the Bolshevik Party and the
> Communist International?), I nevertheless considered, not only
> that the October Revolution had opened a new era in the history of
> mankind (which I still believe), but also that the economic and social
> development of the Soviet Union provided a sort of "model"
> for the building of socialism. The difficulties and contradictions
> accompanying this development seemed to me, despite their serious-
> ness, to be due above all to the special historical conditions of
> Russia. I thought there was no reason why they should reappear
> elsewhere, or should prevent Russia from continuing to advance
> toward socialism and communism.[2]

Bettelheim goes on to explain that economic successes beginning with the five year plans, the triumph over Hitlerism, the
rapidity of postwar recovery, the improvement of the Soviet
standard of living, and aid to socialist China all seemed to confirm
these views, although (he notes) the inequalities which had arisen
in the course of the early plans had shown no tendency to
diminish, but on the contrary had increased. The Twentieth

Congress of the Communist Party of the Soviet Union (1956) seemed to provide further evidence: though it produced no analysis of the difficulties and contradictions which had led to past acts of repression and tended to blame everything on Stalin, still it seemed to indicate that the Soviet Union was embarking on a path of socialist democracy and that the CPUSSR had retained, or regained, the capacity of self-criticism necessary for the rectification of errors.

In reality all this was an illusion. Laying all the blame on Stalin (the personality cult) signified in fact that the CPUSSR had abandoned Marxism and was incapable of tackling the task of transforming the real social relations which had given rise to the evils verbally condemned. "The pseudo explanation given thus fulfilled its task of consolidating the class relations which concentrated economic and political power in the hands of a minority." (p. 11) Contradictions, far from being alleviated, were only deepened. Among them, both in the Soviet Union and in the countries allied to it, was a growing malfunctioning of the economic system. This in turn gave rise to reforms based on assigning a growing role to capitalist forms and criteria in the management of the economy. But this proved to be no remedy, and continuing negative developments far outweighed the positive. The effect on the workers in these countries was clearly seen in the uprisings in the Baltic ports of Poland in December 1970, which had repercussions in the Soviet Union on both workers and leaders. The latter, like their Polish counterparts, reacted in classical ruling-class fashion, making superficial concessions on the one hand and accentuating repression on the other.

Along with these internal developments went a transformation of Soviet foreign policy, characterized by an increasing abandonment of what had once been its socialist features. Brutal, if unsuccessful, pressures were brought to bear on China and Albania to force them to submit to Soviet hegemony; and on the world stage the Soviet Union increasingly played the part of a "great power," entering into both competition and collaboration with the United States as the other great power. The huge armaments race growing out of this situation forced the Soviet Union to devote a far larger share of its productive resources to arms than was true of the United States, placed heavier and heavier burdens on the Soviet people, and finally drove the leaders to seek financial and technical aid from their chief rival. Having reviewed this record, Bettelheim concludes:

> A review of this process of evolution (in which the occupation of Czechoslovakia figures as one moment) caused me to reconsider also the *past* of the Soviet Union, for it is impossible to suppose that the course being followed by that country results merely from the "personal responsibility" of a few leaders. The accession to power of these leaders and their ability to operate the policy I have described are necessarily to be explained by the social relations that now prevail in the USSR, and that took shape over a long preceding period. Hence the need to analyze these relations. (p. 14)

Bettelheim next relates how, in approaching this task, he was influenced by his experiences with, and reflections on, the Cuban and Chinese revolutions, and especially the Cultural Revolution in China. Gradually he had come to reject a version of "Marxism" which had long been dominant in Europe and which Lenin had characterized as "economism," i.e., a theoretical interpretation which unilaterally subordinates the transformation of social relations to the development of the forces of production.* (I should add that until quite recently this kind of economism was as dominant in Marxist circles in the United States as it was in Europe, and probably in most other parts of the world as well.)

---

*As Bettelheim points out in another context, this subordination of the transformation of social relations to the development of the forces of production has typically been conceived of in an extraordinarily narrow (and egregiously un-Marxian) way, in that "forces of production" have been thought of almost exclusively in terms of science, technology, machines, etc., and hardly at all in terms of the workers themselves. The result has been a heavy emphasis on developing the instruments of production with a corresponding neglect of the human agents without which these instruments are so much dead matter. If "forces of production" are interpreted in such a way as to give clear priority to human beings, the conclusion can hardly be avoided that the very idea of separating forces of producton from social relations is a characteristic, and indeed essential, element of bourgeois ideology. Bettelheim is therefore absolutely correct when he says (p. 35) that economism is "the form which bourgeois ideology takes within Marxism." And he adds, with equal justification, that this ideology "has its roots in bourgeois social relations which can disappear only with the disappearance of classes as such."

Early in 1969 Bettelheim finished a manuscript subjecting Soviet society to a critical analysis and demonstrating that "under cover of state ownership, relations of exploitation exist today in the USSR which are similar to those existing in the other capitalist countries, so that it is only the *form* of these relations that is distinctive there." (p. 17) He decided, however, not to publish this text since it was lacking in historical background, and by this time he had become convinced of the necessity of a careful historical analysis:

> It is indeed impossible to understand the Soviet Union's present without relating it to the country's past. It is not enough to show the relations and practices that are dominant today; one must also explain how they have become dominant. One needs therefore to consider how, through what struggles and contradictions, the first country of the dictatorship of the proletariat has become transformed into a country carrying out an imperialist policy, which does not hesitate to send its armed forces into other countries in order to uphold its great-power interests.
>
> Analysis of the transformation that the Soviet Union has undergone is at least as important as analysis of the present situation taken on its own; such an analysis can serve as an invaluable source of instruction, and help other proletarian revolutions to avoid taking the same road and ending up not with socialism, but with a specific form of capitalism just as oppressive and aggressive as the "classical" forms. . . .
>
> The Soviet experience confirms that what is hardest is not the overthrow of the former dominant classes: the hardest task is, first, to destroy the former social relations—upon which a system of exploitation similar to the one supposed to have been overthrown for good can be reconstituted—and then to prevent these relations from being reconstituted on the basis of those elements of the old that still remain present for a long time in the new social relations. (pp. 17–18)

This, then, is the explanation of how it came to pass that Bettelheim launched into the ambitious study of Soviet history of which the volume under consideration is the first fruit.* The

---

*Let me note in passing that this work is *not* the kind of history which professional historians are trained to produce. Quite apart from the fact that Bettelheim had a very specific practical (political) purpose in mind, there is a notable absence of research in original materials such as archives, contemporary periodicals, etc.

remainder of the foreword, being devoted to giving a "general view" of the work as a whole, does not lend itself to neat summarization, and I shall limit myself to brief comments on some of its major themes.

Perhaps the central theme, recurring again and again, is the nature and pervasiveness throughout most of Soviet history of the "rigidified Marxism" *(marxisme figé)* with which, in Bettelheim's view, "one must break in order to restore a true revolutionary character to historical and dialectical materialism." (p. 20) In this connection he lays particular emphasis on erroneous notions regarding (1) the foundations of class relations, (2) the role of productive forces, and (3) the withering away of the state.

With respect to class relations, the primary distortion of Marxism is to treat them as juridically defined and determined. This not only permits but necessitates the conclusion that the abolition of private property in the means of production does away with the bourgeoisie. Thus Bettelheim quotes Stalin's 1936 statement to the Seventh Congress of Soviets: "The capitalist class in the sphere of industry has ceased to exist. The kulak class in the sphere of agriculture has ceased to exist, and the merchants and profiteers in the sphere of trade have ceased to exist. Thus all the exploiting classes have now been eliminated." (p. 21) Furthermore, this view of classes and class relations as being essentially an emanation of the property system means that, short of the restoration of private property in the means of production, no new exploiting class can arise.

The true Marxist position, in contrast, is that classes have their existence in the real relations of production, and that it is only through a transformation of these relations that the class structure can be changed or, in the limiting case, that classes can be abolished. A very large part of Bettelheim's work in this first volume—and perhaps that part will be even larger in subsequent volumes—is devoted to demonstrating that these real relations of production, while undergoing certain modifications, have not been radically transformed in the Soviet Union, and that it has

---

Bettelheim of course makes extensive use of the published speeches and writings of Bolshevik leaders and of official party documents, but for the rest his sources are mostly drawn from the vast monographic literature on the Soviet Union and Soviet history. This specialized literature (largely produced by professional historians) is thus not only essential for analytical works like Bettelheim's but receives its *raison d'être* and justification through them. At least for Marxists *historia gratia historiae* makes no more sense than *ars gratia artis*.

therefore been possible for a new ruling class, which he calls a "state bourgeoisie," to emerge in the place of the old bourgeoisie of Tsarist Russia. I shall return to the question of classes in the Soviet Union in the final section of this essay. Here a final word on the subject: what may be called the juridical theory of classes was by no means a distortion of Marxism peculiar to Stalin and the CPUSSR under his domination. It was also held by many who on other grounds were strongly opposed to Stalin, most notably Trotsky and his followers. To this day the Trotskyists doggedly maintain that the USSR is not and cannot be a class society because there is no private ownership of the means of production.

With respect to the second subject listed above, Bettelheim writes: "A second thesis characteristic of the simplification of Marxism which tended to impose itself during the 1930s in the European sections of the Third International was that of the primacy of the development of the productive forces. This thesis presented the development of the productive forces as the 'driving force of history.' " (p. 23) The great merit of this view from the point of view of the Soviet leaders was that it seemed to provide an explanation of all the troubles and contradictions which the country was experiencing: the forces of production were still too backward and undeveloped to permit an advance to a harmonious, smoothly functioning socialist society. Though the foundation of such a society had been laid through the substitution of state and cooperative ownership for private ownership of the means of production (no more exploiting classes, hence no exploited either), the edifice itself could not be built without a decisive increase and improvement in the productive forces. "Hence the slogans of the period: 'Technique decides everything' and 'Catch up with and surpass the most advanced capitalist countries.' " (p. 26) Though Bettelheim does not say it, this seems to be exactly what the Chinese mean by "putting economics in command"; to this they contrast their own policy of "putting politics in command," by which they mean giving priority to transforming human beings and their relations to each other. This, in turn, involves recognizing that antagonistic classes continue to exist, either actually or potentially, under a proletarian dictatorship (otherwise what is the point of a *class* dictatorship?), and that a policy of class struggle must be persisted in and carried through to the end. It should be added that "putting politics in command" does *not* mean downgrading or neglecting the development of the productive forces: on the contrary, it is the best and, in the final analysis, the only way to develop the productive forces as they need to be developed under socialism and on the road to communism.

Here, as in the case of the theory of classes, Bettelheim shows that the distortion of Marxism was shared by Stalin and his opponents. In particular, Trotsky was a rather more extreme believer in the primacy of productive forces than Stalin. Bettelheim quotes Trotsky as writing: "The strength and stability of regimes are determined in the long run by the relative productivity of their labour. A socialist economy possessing a technique superior to that of capitalism would really be guaranteed in its socialist development for sure—so to speak, automatically." (p. 29) Alas for illusions!

Turning now to the question of the withering away of the state, we find the Soviet theorists confronted with a problem to which they could find no counterpart, let alone solution, in the classical texts of Marxism. According to the latter (Marx, Engels, Lenin), the state as an apparatus of repression (equipped with armed forces, police, jails, etc.) would lose its *raison d'être* and begin to wither away along with, and roughly in proportion to, the abolition of the division of society into exploiting and exploited classes. Since the Soviet state showed no signs of weakening, not to mention disappearing—quite the opposite—this fact was in standing contradiction to the claim that the abolition of private property in the means of production had eliminated class antagonisms. Stalin had a ready answer: the Soviet Union existed in the midst of a hostile capitalist world and the state was now needed to protect the country against the spies, saboteurs, and assassins constantly being sent in by the imperialists in an effort to overthrow the revolutionary regime and restore the old ruling classes to power. To this Bettelheim replies: Why should a gigantic and growing repressive apparatus be needed for this task? Why couldn't it be handled by the masses themselves in a country in which it was really true that no class had any interest in supporting counter-revolutionary activities? Considering the magnitude of the repression, its forms, and the contradictions which characterized it, it is hard to avoid Bettelheim's conclusion that the problem can be comprehended better "when we set these facts in relation not mainly to the activity of foreign spies and the 'slackness of will' of Soviet citizens but to *a class struggle that was both furious and blind.*" (p. 31) Trotsky, also confronted with the same problem (since he too accepted the thesis of the disappearance of exploiting and exploited classes), offered a different, purely economic explanation of the continued existence of the state. As long as the development of the productive forces remains at a low level, what Engels had called the "struggle for individual existence" goes on, pitting people against each other and requiring a state to prevent social disintegration. This explanation is evidently perfectly compatible with Trotsky's views on the primacy of productive forces noted above.

Having reviewed the three basic distortions of Marxism which characterized Soviet thought, both official and oppositional, during the 1920s and 1930s (with respect to the existence of classes, the role of the productive forces, and the withering away of the state), Bettelheim proceeds:

> This flashback should help the reader to understand the quasi-impossibility for those who accepted the theses discussed (and until recently that meant, in Europe at least, the overwhelming majority of all who recognized that the October Revolution had opened a new era in the history of mankind) to carry out a Marxist analysis of Soviet society, since essential to such an analysis would be not to shut one's eyes to class relations and the effects of the class struggle, but on the contrary, to perceive that here are relations and a struggle which are of decisive importance, and destined to remain so until a classless, communist society has been built. (p. 32)

He immediately adds, however, that "this review of the past still fails to provide an answer to the following question: Why did the economistic problematic, of which the theses discussed above form parts, play for so long (and why does it still play) its specific ideological role?" (p. 32)*

---

*I confess that I cannot make much sense out of the way Bettelheim—like many other French writers—uses the term "problématique," which now seems to be commonly taken over into English translations as well. Sometimes it seems to be meant in the sense of an "interrelated set of problems," which I find a good and useful concept. But I have marked numerous other occurences of the term where it seems to be the equivalent of "concept," "theory," "approach," or something similar. The trouble is that I am never quite sure what is meant.

Bettelheim doesn't really answer this question in the few remaining pages of the foreword, but he does provide some helpful clues. He notes that economistic thinking takes on various forms in different times and different social situations, sometimes appearing in a "rightist" guise (e.g., social democracy) and sometimes in a "leftist" guise (e.g., Trotskyism). The problem in any given case is not only to recognize the economistic essence but to link it to the position and interests of a particular class and/or group within a class. What may be called the classical form of economism within the working-class movement was the revisionism which, in fact if not always in words, pervaded the German Social Democratic Party in the decades before World War I.* Calling this a "rightist" form of economism, Bettelheim observes that:

> it was connected with the existence within this party of a powerful political and trade-union apparatus which became integrated with the German state machine. The heads of this powerful apparatus were able to delude themselves that a steady increase in their organizational activity and pressure for workers' demands would eventually create the conditions for capitalism to be overthrown. They were all the more attached to this illusion because, by indulging it, they could strengthen their own positions in the German labor movement without, apparently, having to incur the risks inherent in revolutionary activity. (p. 36)

As examples of "leftist" (or, as Bettelheim also calls them, "rightist-leftist") economism, the author cites tendencies which manifested themselves in the Bolshevik Party in the period of "war communism." One such tendency envisaged a direct passage to communism through rigid state controls over everything, including the workers. Another in effect wanted the workers'

---

*I have argued elsewhere that German revisionism was in reality the continental version of English Fabianism. The direct link between the two was none other than Eduard Bernstein, the chief theorist of German revisionism, who spent years of exile in England in close contact with the Fabians. When he got back to Germany, he wrote his famous revisionist tract (English title: *Evolutionary Socialism*) which, apart from the use of Marxian terms (mandatory in the German environment), was entirely in the Fabian tradition. See Paul M. Sweezy, "Fabian Political Economy," in *The Present as History* (New York: Monthly Review Press, 1953), esp. pp. 305–316.

economic organizations (the trade unions) to take control over the state. In reality, Bettelheim writes:

> these two conceptions both deny the decisive role of the ideological and political class struggle and the necessity (in order to carry this struggle through to victory) of a Marxist-Leninist party guided by a correct political line. The first conception tends to substitute state coercion for political and ideological leadership of the proletariat, while the second tends to replace this leadership by the activity of the trade unions. (p. 35)

Bettelheim links these new forms of economism to the growth, after the October Revolution, within the Bolshevik Party of "a stratum of administrators and of business, planning, and financial officials," with their own particular interests and outlook. "As will be seen, these new forms assumed a rightist or leftist appearance depending on the course of the class struggle and on the characteristics of those strata of the workers that could provide a social basis for them." (p. 35)

What is common to all forms of economism, whether rightist or leftist, is that they all objectively favor the short-term or medium-term outlook and interests of a particular segment or segments of the population, and hence tend to strengthen and perpetuate social divisions. Marxism, on the other hand, is quintessentially the body of thought which identifies the *long-term* interests of the *whole* population and provides a guide to their realization. These long-term interests do not coincide with the short- or medium-term interests of any existing class or stratum, not even of the proletariat, since their essence is precisely the elimination of *all* existing classes and other social divisions which generate conflicts of interest. Proletarian revolution is thus not a process by which the proletariat seeks to improve its own lot as a class, but one by which it seeks to do away with itself as a class, which of course involves doing away with all other classes as well. The leading role which Marxism assigns to the proletariat stems from two undeniable facts: First, that it is *necessarily and unavoidably* the victim of exploitation and dehumanization under capitalism and can escape this fate only by revolution carried through to the end; and second, that potentially it has the *power* to overthrow the rule of capital. But these facts provide no guarantee that the proletariat will understand its situation and act accordingly. For that, it must first grasp and assimilate Marxism, which it can do only through political organization and unremitting struggle, under the guidance of a genuinely Marxist vanguard party. Since this is at best a very long, complicated, and difficult process, it is obvious that innumerable opportunities to make mistakes, to get side-tracked, and to take wrong turns will present themselves. And there will always, or at least for a very long time, be elements rooted in the past, ready and anxious to take advantage of errors and false steps to turn the clock back and reestablish or strengthen positions of privilege and relations of exploitation. This is where the various forms of economism come into the picture: they are the oversimplifications and distortions of Marxism which permit these elements to pose as revolutionaries—and often to believe quite sincerely that they are revolutionaries—while actually perform-ing the work of counterrevolution. The task which Bettelheim set himself, and which he has to a large extent succeeded in accom-plishing, is to explain how and why economism triumphed over Marxism in the Soviet Union, leading to the abandonment of the socialist road and finally to the full restoration of a bourgeois society of a new kind.

In the last ten pages of his foreword Bettelheim presents a very helpful preliminary sketch of Stalin's role in this process. Stalin neither originated nor forced upon the Bolshevik Party the economistic version of Marxism which came into full flower after the introduction of the First Five Year Plan. In fact he accurately reflected and expressed ideas which were widely held at all levels of the party, but his great prestige as leader and chief spokes-man of the Russian Revolution after Lenin's death gave added weight and authority to his formulations and pronouncements. Bettelheim argues, correctly I think, that Stalin's prestige derived not so much from his official position as secretary of the party as from the fact that in certain important respects he upheld posi-tions which Lenin had taken, or begun to take in his last years, and which were in accord with the feelings and desires of the great majority of the party's membership. This was above all true of his vigorous championing of the socialism-in-one-country doctrine, which set tasks for the party other than just hanging on to power and hoping for better days, and in fact set in motion changes and transformations of vast magnitude and historical significance. The result, to be sure, was not the construction of socialism in the USSR, but the country did develop the industrial and military strength to defeat Hitlerism and to make what was probably a decisive contribution to preventing a successful imperialist intervention against the Chinese Revolution when it was still very weak and vulnerable. These are gigantic achievements which on a world-historical scale may well be reckoned as outweighing in importance for the world revolution the negative effects of the turning away from socialism in the Soviet Union. And while, as Bettelheim rightly says, it was the heroism and sacrifices of the Soviet people which made these achievements possible, Stalin inevitably got much of the credit, plus the enormous prestige which went with it.

Bettelheim notes that economism had always been stronger in the advanced capitalist countries than in Russia and that it is therefore not surprising that the Soviet experience served to entrench it even more deeply in the worker and communist movements of Western Europe. But he also emphasizes that by now the economistic way of thinking about the construction of socialism has been severely shaken. Two factors have been of decisive importance here.

The first is the experience of the Chinese Revolution, which has shown that a low level of the development of the productive forces is not an insuperable obstacle to the socialist transformation of social relations and does not necessarily entail a process of "primitive accumulation" and the aggravation of inequalities; that it is self-defeating to try to build the material bases of socialism first, while putting off until later the task of developing compatible social relations; that the socialist transformation of the superstructure must accompany the development of the productive forces, and that this transformation effectively conditions the socialist character of economic development.

The second factor which has shaken the economistic way of thinking derives directly from Soviet experience. The low level of the productive forces used to be available as an "explanation" for all the contradictions, difficulties, and failures of the USSR.

But this is no longer so. The Soviet Union has become the world's second industrial power, and even leads in some fields of science and technology. At the same time the phenomena which economism tried to explain by the backward state of the USSR and which were thus believed to have a merely transitory character, far from disappearing have become more deeply entrenched. Here we must quote in full an eloquent passage which all who consider themselves to be socialists and Marxists should study carefully and take to heart:

> The privileges that, when they arose in the recent past, were regarded as having been imposed by the conditions of the moment, by the needs of accumulation, are today officially recognized elements in the system of social relations within which it is claimed that the Soviet Union is "building the material foundations of communism." For the Soviet Communist Party there is no question of dismantling this system: on the contrary, it seeks to reinforce it. There is no question of allowing the Soviet workers to exercise collective control over the utilization of the means of production, over the way current production is used, or over the activity of the party and its members. The factories are run by managers whose relations with "their" workers are relations of command, and who are responsible only to their superiors. Agricultural enterprises are run in practically similar ways. In general, the direct producers have no right to express themselves—or rather, they can do so only when ritually called upon to approve decisions or "proposals" worked out independently of them in the "higher circles" of the state and the party.
>
> The rules governing the management of Soviet enterprises are to an increasing degree copied from those of the "advanced" capitalist countries, and many Soviet managers go for training to the business schools of the United States and Japan. What was supposed to give rise to increasingly socialist relations has instead produced relations that are essentially capitalist, so that behind the screen of "economic plans," it is the laws of capitalist accumulation, and so of profit, that decide how the means of production are utilized.
>
> The producers are still wage earners working to valorize the means of production, with the latter functioning as collective capital managed by a state bourgeoisie. This bourgeoisie forms, like any other capitalist class, the corps of "functionaries of capital," to use Marx's definition of the capitalist class. The party in power offers to

the working people only an indefinite renewal of these social relations. It is, in practice, the party of the "functionaries of capital,"
acting as such on both the national and international planes.

For anyone who faces the facts, life itself has dispelled any hopes
one might have cherished for the consolidation—and, a fortiori,
the extension—of the gains of the proletarian revolution in the
Soviet Union. Today we need to try and understand why these
hopes have been dashed, so as to appreciate what the USSR has
become, and by way of what transformations. These are two of the
aims of this work, which I have thought it necessary to pursue for
several reasons. (pp. 44–45)

The final section of the foreword tells us what these reasons
are. First, there are many people who do not want to look facts in
the face. They continue to identify the Soviet Union with socialism.
This weighs heavily on working-class struggles, especially in the
industrialized countries. The example of the USSR does not
attract the workers in these countries, and the "explanations"
which the Communist Party leaders try to present as to why it will
be "different" there than in the Soviet Union ("The French are
not Russians," etc.) convince only those who want to be convinced; the others are repelled by the equation of the USSR
with socialism.

The second reason, undoubtedly related to the first, is the
urgent need to expose and struggle against economism, which
dominates the ideology of the working-class movements in the
advanced countries (and is present, often in a "leftist" form, in
the underdeveloped countries as well). The Soviet Union shows
most clearly where these doctrines lead, and the analysis of its
experiences thus constitutes an indispensable "negative lesson"
for those who want to struggle for socialism while ridding themselves of these pernicious doctrines. Those who especially need to
master this lesson are of course the militants of the revisionist
parties who have become effectively paralyzed by their inability to
comprehend the Soviet Union. This paralysis is by now so deep
that it appears to foreshadow a rethinking of the whole question
of reformist and revisionist practices. Nothing could be more
central to such a process than an effort to understand the past and
the present of the Soviet Union. The alternative appears to be the

futile confinement of proletarian and popular struggles to the familiar triad: electoralist reformism, trade union struggles supposedly independent of political organization, and spontaneism.

Fortunately, there are factors at work which give grounds for hope. One is the unprecedented crisis which the world capitalist system is going through: economically it has taken the initial form of an international monetary crisis of vast proportions; ideologically it is marked by refusal on the part of important sectors of the population in the advanced countries (especially working-class youths, students, and women) to continue accepting the forms of subjection which capitalism imposes upon them; politically there is the upsurge of national and revolutionary struggles in many of the underdeveloped countries. Another hopeful factor in the situation is the positive lesson which—in contrast to the Soviet failure—can be drawn from the construction of socialism in China:

> There, life—meaning the struggle of the masses, led by a genuine Marxist-Leninist party—has shown how to solve the problems presented by the socialist transformation of social relations. Marxism-Leninism has thus found fresh vigor and clarified a series of questions which could indeed be clarified only through social practice. (pp. 47–48)

Finally, Bettelheim concludes on a note of tribute to the working people of the USSR. They have suffered grave setbacks, "but the struggle of the proletariat and the peasantry continues, and will inevitably—after delays and through ups and downs about which it is futile to speculate—lead the working people of the Soviet republics to restore their power and resume the building of socialism." (p. 48)

(November 1974)

5
THE NATURE
OF SOVIET SOCIETY—
PART 2

Overthrowing the old and building the new

Every real revolution has two aspects: overthrowing the old structure of power and building the new social order. The former opens the way for the latter but does not guarantee that the positive task will be successfully accomplished. This depends on the strength and understanding of the new elements which gain power through the revolutionary process—relative of course to the obstacles to be overcome and the opposition offered by the defeated but still far from dead supporters of the old society. I think it is a fair summary of Bettelheim's main thesis that in the Russian case the revolutionary forces were too weak and (unavoidably) too lacking in understanding based on relevant historical experience to solve the enormously complicated and difficult problems involved in replacing the old order by a new, genuinely socialist society.

The weakness of the Russian revolutionary forces stemmed from many sources. Their social base of course was the urban industrial working class, and their leadership was provided by the Bolshevik Party. The problem was not that these forces, so based and so led, were lacking in revolutionary spirit or experience. If that had been the case, the October Revolution would never have taken place at all. The trouble was that the proletariat was small relative to the population as a whole, and the Bolsheviks had few links and almost no influence in the countryside where the vast majority of Russians lived. Added to this basic situation were the terrible losses and disruption of the civil war years (1917–1921). This point is so important to an understanding of what happened in the USSR and it has been so generally neglected or underestimated that a lengthy quotation seems called for:

> By the beginning of the 1920s the Russian proletariat had suffered a terrible bloodletting. It had literally melted away during the civil war, and this process was continuing at the outset of the NEP. Thus, in 1922, the number of employed workers was less than half the prewar figure—4.6 million instead of 11 million in 1913, within the same frontiers, and of these 4.6 million, only 2 million were employed in industry, 1.2 million being agricultural laborers.
>
> The active working class was not only reduced numerically but also greatly altered in its composition. Many of the most militant workers had fallen at the front. Others had been absorbed into the machinery of the party, the trade unions, and the state. Others, especially in the big industrial centers, had left the ranks of the working class, owing to unemployment or the food shortage, and gone back to their native villages. At the same time, men and women of bourgeois and petty bourgeois origin, who were usually hostile to the dictatorship of the proletariat, had made their way into the ranks of the working class so as to take advantage of the higher rations available to manual workers, or to conceal their class origin.
>
> Amidst a population of 136 million, of whom about half were of working age, the number of those who made up the active nucleus of the new ruling class were thus small; and this was so even if one adds to the workers actually employed in 1922 the former workers who were ready to go back to their old places in production. The solidity of the proletarian dictatorship was not mainly determined by the relative weight of the working class, but, above all, by its class organization and by its ability to exercise ideological and political leadership of the masses. (p. 172)

In these conditions it is obvious that the Bolshevik leadership, even where it was strongest and most experienced, lacked the resources to replace the old Tsarist administration and bureaucracy with a new revolutionary apparatus: while in the countryside where it was weakest, it could do almost nothing to influence the course of events. The result was that it had to struggle along as best it could with the sprawling, inefficient, corrupt state machine inherited from the past. It is crucial to understand, moreover, that not only did this inherited state machine have the qualities just listed; it also had an indelible class character. In its essence it was a *bourgeois* state machine, built up over many generations, possessed of a dyed-in-the-wool bourgeois mentality, wedded to bourgeois ways of doing things, and profoundly hostile to the ideology and purposes of the revolutionary power it was forced to serve. As evidence of the latter and reflecting the class nature of the state machine, Bettelheim cites (p. 526) an inquiry conducted in the summer of 1922 which showed that only 9 percent of the old officials and 13 percent of the new ones were favorable to the Soviet regime.

It was absolutely unavoidable that this government apparatus, which the Bolsheviks were obliged to add to and expand as the state assumed new functions previously reserved to the private sector, should be and remain a fertile field for the preservation and resurgence of bourgeois relations not only within its own confines but also throughout Soviet society. And ironically, not a few of the measures taken by the leadership to control and counter these developments tended to have the opposite effect. In particular, honest revolutionaries assigned to positions in the state apparatus with a view to implementing officially adopted policies were more often than not assimilated by their new environment and transformed into ordinary bourgeois bureaucrats. This does not mean that they deliberately betrayed the trust put in them. On the contrary, it is probably safe to assume that in most cases they tried their best to do what was expected of them but that, even in so doing, they acquired the ways of thinking and acting of those around them. Working-class men and women might resist these pressures longer than others, but it is of course a fallacy to assume that class origin is a lasting determinant of ideology and behavior. In this connection, Lenin, who was extremely sensitive to this range of problems—far more so than most of his colleagues in the Bolshevik leadership—had recourse to a telling analogy. In Bettelheim's words, he drew

an analogy between the situation of the Bolshevik Party, which occupied the leading positions in the state but could not really govern, and that of a conquering people which had apparently subjugated another people but, in the long run, though still occupying the latter's territory, became subject to it, because "the vanquished nation," being "more civilised," "imposes its culture upon the conquerer."*

Measures, apart from placing trusted revolutionaries in important state positions (in the Red Army this took the form of the political commissar system), were also instituted to deal with the hostile/bourgeois character of the state apparatus. A People's Commissariat for State Control was established in 1919 under Stalin's directorship, and this was transformed into the Workers' and Peasants' Inspection *(Rabkrin)*, also under Stalin, a year later. But this institution did not escape the fate of other government agencies, becoming merely one branch of the bureaucracy pitted against others. Bettelheim quotes Lenin as writing, shortly before his death (in that truly remarkable essay "Better Fewer, But Better"), that the Workers' and Peasants' Inspection "does not at present enjoy the slightest authority." (p. 274) And indeed it is clear from this and other writings of the last year or so of his life that this question of the condition of the machinery of state (which elsewhere in "Better Fewer, But Better" he called "deplorable, not to say disgusting") was of growing concern almost to the point of becoming an obsession with Lenin.[1] It is interesting to speculate on what he might have tried to do to remedy the situation if he had lived and been able to resume active leadership of party and state. It is of course impossible to be sure, but it is by no means fanciful to surmise that sooner or later he might have attempted to stir up a mass movement to purge and control the governing apparatus similar to the Cultural Revolution in China in the 1960s. As E. H. Carr has written: "If Lenin was driven by practical necessities to recognize a constantly growing concentration of authority, there is no evidence that he wavered in his belief in the antidote of 'direct democracy.' "[2] Such an operation would obviously have been impossible in the chaotic situation of the early 1920s, but it might have been seriously considered in the relative calm of a few years later.

---

*P. 296, citing Lenin's political report to the Eleventh Congress of the Bolshevik Party (March 1922). This analogy was taken up a year later and developed in a most interesting way by Bukharin in a text which is quoted at considerable length by Bettelheim on pp. 297–299.

Maintenance of bourgeois relations in the economy

It was not only in the state apparatus that bourgeois relations and bourgeois attitudes continued to prevail after the October Revolution. This is obvious in the case of agriculture where the revolution (and later the New Economic Policy) established and strengthened a regime of small peasant ownership which in turn set the stage for a characteristic capitalist accumulation process and the flourishing of a class of rich peasants or kulaks. No less important was the maintenance of essentially capitalist relations in industry, transportation, and finance, i.e., the branches of the economy which were transferred to state ownership.

Here it is necessary to insist that what is crucial is not the form of property ownership but the real relations among the groups and individuals involved in the processes of production and distribution. Public ownership opens the way, and is a necessary prerequisite, to the transformation of these relations. But taken by itself it neither constitutes nor guarantees such a transformation, which can come about only as the result of a long and difficult struggle. In the Soviet Union not only has this struggle not been carried through, it was never even begun. Bettelheim makes this point most succinctly in his recent book on industrial organization in China:

> The principles of the absolute authority of the director, of the privileged role of experts and specialists, and of the need to stress bonuses and material rewards are not confined to current management practice in the Soviet Union. These principles were implemented in Russia under the difficult conditions that prevailed after the October Revolution, especially during the period of War Communism. They were maintained under the New Economic Policy, and received a strong impetus during the period of rapid industrialization that followed in the wake of the first five-year plans.[3]

The principles in question are of course those which derive from the kind of hierarchical division of labor which lies at the heart of the capitalist mode of production. Lenin was quite aware that their implementation by the Bolshevik government was in no sense a move toward socialism. In fact he interpreted the decision to strengthen the authority and raise the pay of specialists in precisely the opposite sense:

It is clear that this measure not only implies the cessation—in a certain field and to a certain degree—of the offensive against capital (for capital is not a sum of money, but a definite social relation); it is also a *step backward* on the part of our socialist Soviet state power, which from the very outset proclaimed and pursued the policy of reducing high salaries to the level of the wages of the average worker.[4]

The trouble is, as Bettelheim adds, that this step backward was never followed by a step forward. And he concludes this brief discussion of Soviet development in this field—which in effect summarizes a much more extensive analysis in the book under review—as follows:

Lenin's views may have corresponded to the requirements of a specific stage of the Russian Revolution, but once adopted (between 1918 and 1922) and implemented, they were never abandoned. On the contrary, the weight and authority of the factory director and of the factory party secretary—authority which is not subject to review by the workers—have become more powerful over the years. In fact, the consolidation in the factory of the relations of authority and command between administration, cadres, specialists, and technicians on the one hand and the direct producers on the other, has provided fertile ground for the growth of Soviet revisionism.[5]

One could go further and say that the consolidation of these relations not only provided fertile ground for the growth of Soviet revisionism but, together with the maintenance of bourgeois relations in the apparatuses of government, constituted the very essence of Soviet revisionism. Lenin, and doubtless many others in the Bolshevik leadership in the early years of the Russian Revolution, understood what was going on but lacked the power and resources to take effective countermeasures. Later on, when conditions were more favorable for a struggle to transform the bourgeois social relations which had been inherited from the past and had perforce been maintained and even strengthened in the difficult years of civil war and reconstruction, even the party leadership itself lost the understanding and will which would have been necessary to launch such a struggle. It was in the course of this process that revisionism became not only the day-to-day practice but also the official ideology of the Soviet Union. This presumably will be one of the central themes of the forthcoming second and third volumes of Bettelheim's work.

Some problems of theory and method

Class and class struggle. The theory of classes with which Bettelheim operates seems to me to be unobjectionable as far as it goes. It is well summed up in the following quotation from Lenin:

> Classes are large groups of people differing from each other by the place they occupy in a historically determined system of social production, by their relation (in most cases fixed and formulated by law) to the means of production, by their role in the social organisation of labour, and, consequently, by the dimensions of the share of social wealth of which they dispose and the mode of acquiring it. (p. 139)

Like all brief definitions or characterizations, however, this one has its weaknesses. It makes possible a comprehesive picture of a given society's class structure at a particular moment in time, but it is of little help when we come to analyze the dynamic aspects of a class system: what determines an individual's position in the class structure and changes in that position in the course of a lifetime, the ways in which classes perceive their interests and act to further them, how they are organized and interact, and so on—the list could be extended almost indefinitely. I am far from believing in the existence of a theory of classes adequate to the study of all these difficult problems, but I do think that certain additions to the Lenin-Bettelheim theory can be useful in clarifying some of the most important issues presented by transitional societies like post-1917 Russia and post-1949 China. In particular I would stress the point that the appropriate unit of class membership is not the individual but the family. In a class society everyone is born into a definite class position, and this fact largely determines his or her life chances. This does not mean, however, that individuals must remain in the classes into which they are born. They can move up or down in the class structure in ways and through channels which are historically specific to each social formation.

Mobile individuals take their families with them or start new families in the new class position, though it usually requires at least two generations for a downwardly mobile family to accept, or for an upwardly mobile family to be accepted into, its new class position.

In "normal" times the bourgeois class structure is buttressed and stabilized by property laws enforced by a state apparatus designed and trained to preserve the system and promote the interests of its beneficiaries (i.e., the property owners who thus constitute the ruling class or, if significantly different kinds of property are involved, the ruling classes). The defining characteristic of the revolution is that it overthrows the state and changes the property system. In accordance with what has been said above, we know that this does not mean that the real relations of production which determine the class composition of society undergo a comparable alteration. But by removing the protector and stabilizer of these relations of production and putting in power the representatives of a class with interests opposed to those of the former ruling class, the revolution poses the possibility of a change in the real relations of production and at the same time introduces a degree of fluidity and uncertainty into the class system without precedent in the preceding period. Mobility in both directions is dramatically increased. Many property owners are not only dispossessed but removed from positions of authority and often driven into exile or physically liquidated. Conversely, many workers are propelled into positions of authority in the hierarchical division of labor. These movements may even be on such a massive scale as to give the appearance of the virtual elimination of the old class system and the beginning of the end of classes altogether. But a look below the surface, at the real relations of production, will show that this appearance is illusory: fundamental changes at this level can come about only slowly and as a result of a long and complicated struggle, and even then they may not come about at all.

Bettelheim—and in this he follows the Chinese—calls this a class struggle. I think this is basically correct, but at the same time I think it is important to understand that it is a class struggle with a number of special features which differentiate it from the kind of class struggle we are most familiar with from the history of capitalism.

It is of course true that in one sense the familiar type of class struggle continues after the revolution. The overthrown ruling class always tries to make a comeback through organizing counter-revolution, usually with the help of its class counterparts in other countries where no revolution has taken place. But with the passage of time and the dying off of the old ruling class, this form of class struggle diminishes in importance to the point of practical insignificance. It is certainly not what Bettelheim has in mind when he writes of class struggles in the USSR or China, neither of which is seriously threatened by whatever remnants of the old ruling classes may still be in existence. What he does have in mind is a much more complex phenomenon, i.e., the efforts of those in positions of privilege and authority in the post-revolutionary state apparatus and economy (including professional, educational, and cultural institutions) to hold onto their positions *and* to find new ways of stabilizing, protecting, and perpetuating their favored status in society.

It is here that the fact that the family rather than the individual is the basic unit of class membership takes on special significance. If everyone at birth had an equal chance of reaching a given position in the social structure, classes as we know them would not exist at all. But—and this is the crucial point—such a situation of full equality of life chances is inconceivable so long as differences of income, status, and authority still persist. The cards are stacked in favor of children born into families with relatively privileged positions, and this is as true of societies calling themselves socialist as it is of capitalist or feudal societies. It is therefore no accident that the class struggle in post-revolutionary societies tends to focus on the real inequalities which divide families occupying different positions in the social division of labor. These inequalities are not only or perhaps even primarily a matter of income: a considerable range of income differentials would be compatible with all children having substantially equal life chances. More important are a number of other factors which are less well defined, less visible, and impossible to quantify: the advantages of coming from a more "cultured" home environment, differential access to educational opportunities, the possession of "connections" in the circles of those holding positions of power and prestige, feelings of strength and self-confidence which children absorb from their parents—the list could be expanded and elaborated. These intangible factors are all operative in bourgeois society too, in which they interact with large differentials in income and property ownership. Where the latter have been eliminated, or greatly reduced, the intangibles assume even greater importance. They become the main protective walls of privilege, of the still surviving system of bourgeois class relations; and those who live behind them (with exceptions of course) seek to strengthen them, to give them official sanction, and ultimately to confer on them the crowning badge of legitimacy—conceivably even in a new legal system of property relations.

Those occupying privileged positions and seeking to fortify them and perpetuate them in institutional form constitute one of the protagonists in the post-revolutionary class struggle. The other of course is the masses of workers and peasants whose interest is not to defend their class position at all but to eliminate the differences (between manual and mental labor, between town and country, between agriculture and industry, between the sexes, among others) that constitute the objective basis of a class system, and (as a necessary part of this process) to negate the social and ideological barriers which serve to preserve and justify the continued existence of these differences. The struggle between these two protagonists is necessarily a long and complicated one which takes on many forms and disguises. Here I will only note that one of the principal arenas is bound to be the ruling party itself, with both sides professing the party's official revolutionary ideology and each seeking to interpret and implement it in a way favorable to its own purposes. In China this is the basis and substance of the "two-line struggle" which has characterized the Chinese Communist Party's history since 1949 and which reached a climax, for the time being at any rate, in the Cultural Revolution of the late 1960s. We know a lot about this struggle in China since much of it has been in the open and the issues became increasingly clear in the course of the Sino-Soviet dispute and the Cultural Revolution itself. We know a good deal less in the case of the Soviet Union, and much that we may think we know is of dubious reliability, partly owing to the brutal suppression of all opposition during the Stalin period and the systematic falsification of Soviet history, including that of the CPUSSR, then and later. But an added reason for our ignorance of post-revolutionary class struggles in the Soviet Union is that the kinds of Marxism which were dominant in the period of the Second and Third Internationals were heavily infected with a crude "economism" and, as a result, provided a totally inadequate theoretical framework for analyzing and understanding the historically novel forms of society ushered in by successful proletarian revolutions.[6] Bettelheim, basing himself largely on the practical and theoretical achievements of the People's Republic of China, has begun the task of remedying this state of ignorance. We look forward eagerly to additional enlightenment in the volumes still to come.

Marx, Engels, Lenin, and history. Bettelheim has a strong tendency to surround Marx, Engels, and Lenin with an aura of infallibility: they alone among their contemporaries saw things in their true light and drew conclusions as applicable to future events as to those of the past or of their own time. This is especially true of the whole phenomenon of economism which, as readers should be aware by now, I fully agree with Bettelheim is of enormous importance. He treats economism as a grave distortion of the doctrines consistently expounded in the writings of Marx, Engels, and Lenin. Lenin, to be sure, was obliged by overriding objective circumstances to make certain concessions to economistic ways of thinking—as in the case of the relations between managers and workers, mentioned above—but as Bettelheim sees it these concessions were always forced on Lenin and did not reflect ideas which he himself entertained, still less ideas he might have got from Marx or Engels.

This position seems to me both wrong and unhistorical. I could cite passages in Lenin's writings which I think reflect economistic thinking, but to deal with the matter this way would be to risk missing the main point, which is that Marx and Engels themselves made many statements in a variety of contexts which either articulate economistic views or can quite reasonably be interpreted in an economistic sense. As the prime example of the latter I would point to Marx's preface to the *Critique of Political Economy,* which contains by far the most famous and frequently quoted formulation of the doctrine of historical materialism. By saying that the preface can reasonably be interpreted in an economistic sense I do not mean to imply that economism was the dominant theme in Marx's thinking. Quite the contrary: I believe that for the most part his teachings were informed by the ideas succinctly set forth in the *Theses on Feuerbach* which are as thoroughly anti-economistic as anything in the writings of Mao Tsetung. But like most (perhaps all) great thinkers, Marx was far from 100 percent consistent in everything he said or wrote. There were economistic elements in his thinking which sometimes (e.g., in popular or propagandistic writings) received quite explicit expression. That these elements were emphasized and exaggerated by his followers in the half century after his death, often to the exclusion of other more representative and more important tendencies in his think-ing, was of course not his fault, and neither was it an accident. Rather it was in accordance with the ideological and political needs of the reformist working-class movements which flour-ished in the industrialized countries in the period of emerging monopoly capitalism. The Russian movement, growing up in a situation much more favorable to revolution, was less affected by economism, but it would have been most surprising if the Russians had not been influenced in this, as in other matters, by the Western Europeans. Lenin, the most consistently revolu-tionary of the Russians, was the least influenced by economism, but he was not completely immune. It was only in China, where of all countries in the world conditions were most favorable for revolution, that Marxism could finally be purged of its (essentially bourgeois) economistic taint. Now that this great and necessary task has been accomplished, dialectical and historical materialism can and will, in Bettelheim's words, "reestablish contact with what I believe to be the revolutionary content of historical and dialectical materialism." (p. 19)

It seems to me that this perspective enables us to view the development of Marxism as a grand historical process integrally linked with the development of world capitalism in its final phase of maturity and decline. And it enables us to avoid the artificiality of treating the great figures in the development of Marxism as some sort of suprahistorical geniuses.

The nature of Soviet society—a last word. In this first volume of his new work Bettelheim does not say very much about the nature of the society which exists in the Soviet Union today, and what he does say is understandably cautious. He is clear that it is a class society. The two main classes are the state bourgeoisie and the proletariat. The former existed in Lenin's time but had not yet consolidated its hold on political power. Since then it has not only strengthened its control over government and economic apparatuses; it has also permeated the Communist Party both ideologically and numerically, and has thus put an end to its ambiguous position as an unwilling and unreliable instrument of the dictatorship of the proletariat. The position of the proletariat, conversely, has deteriorated from that of a class holding a monopoly of state power—on the uses of which, however, as we have seen, there were severe limitations—to a position similar to that of the proletariat in capitalist countries at a comparable stage of economic development.* The Soviet proletariat remains an exploited class forced to sell its labor power to acquire the means of livelihood and lacking any possibility to control the processes or the products of its labor. And the Soviet state bourgeoisie is of course just as much an exploiting class as is, for example, the private-property-owning bourgeoisie of the United States.

Under these circumstances Bettelheim believes that it is necessary to classify the Soviet Union as a capitalist society, but he is careful to add the qualification "of a particular type." (p. 46) Two pages earlier, however, there is a statement which seems considerably to weaken the force of this qualification: "What was supposed to give rise to increasingly socialist relations has instead produced relations that are essentially capitalist, so that behind the screen of 'economic plans,' it is the laws of capitalist accumulation, and so of profit, that decide how the means of production

---

*This is not to deny that there are differences. The Soviet workers have not lost all the gains they made in their period of political ascendancy, e.g., in such matters as job security, health care, etc. On the other hand, the restrictions on their rights of organization and expression are more severe than in capitalist countries with bourgeois democratic regimes.

are utilized." (p. 44) If, as this suggests, economic plans are really nothing but a cover for the laws of capitalist accumulation, then it would seem that the particularity of the Soviet system is limited to the formal question of whether the bourgeoisie owns the means of production directly or through its state (a form of bourgeois ownership which of course is also widespread in traditional capitalist countries). It would likewise seem to follow that efforts by the Soviet state bourgeoisie, which I for one think are quite likely sooner or later to move in the direction of increasing the sphere of private ownership of the means of production, would not have much effect on the functioning of the system.

These contentions and inferences may be correct. But I have to say that nothing in the way of factual evidence or theoretical argumentation presented by Bettelheim in this book, or that I have seen elsewhere, persuades me. So far as I am concerned, at any rate, these questions are still wide open. I very much hope that this will no longer be the case after the appearance of the final two volumes of *Class Struggles in the USSR*.

(January 1975)

6
THEORY AND PRACTICE
IN THE MAO PERIOD

Marxism grows and develops through the historical experience of class struggles and their reflection in the thoughts of leaders and participants. The two greatest periods and sources of such advance have been the Russian and Chinese revolutions. While it is of course much too soon to come to any final conclusions, the death of a great leader like Mao Tsetung inevitably marks a turning point and invites consideration of what has been accomplished during his lifetime.

When the time comes to attempt an overall evaluation of the Mao period, it may well be concluded that its most important contribution to the advance of Marxism was to break what may be called the tyranny of the Soviet model. The very foundation of this model was "primitive socialist accumulation" at the expense of the peasantry, and its dominant thrust was the building up of heavy industry while concomitantly downgrading the development of light industry and the production of consumer goods.* The application of this model had (and has) many implications: the ending of all hope of an effective worker-peasant alliance and hence (in countries with peasant majorities) the necessity of a severely repressive state. And this in turn meant the renunciation of any possibility of transforming social relations in the direction of communism. In the Marxist orthodoxy of the Stalin period—

---

*The term "primitive socialist accumulation" was Evgeny Preobrazhensky's, but it was far more appropriate to the Stalinist practice than to the relatively mild program advocated by Preobrazhensky himself.

from the 1920s to the 1950s—this problem, to the extent that it was not dealt with in a purely propagandistic way, was put off until some future time when the forces of production would presumably have developed to the point of making general abundance a reality. In this way, development of the forces of production was turned into a sort of universal panacea for all the ills and contradictions of society, and from this it followed that for a socialist society the highest and overriding objective for the foreseeable future must be the most rapid attainable development of the forces of production.*

In the first years after they came to power, the Chinese Communists set out to follow the Soviet model but soon discovered that it put demands on the agricultural sector which could not be met. In a similar situation in the 1920s the Russians decided to squeeze the needed surplus out of the peasants, with the fateful consequences noted above. Quite apart from any reluctance on the part of the Chinese leadership to follow this course, the option did not exist as a realistic possibility. Unlike in the Russian case, the surplus to be squeezed out of the peasantry was simply not there.[1] A different course had to be adopted. And it was here that Maoist ideas, based on long years in governing the border regions and conducting the wars against the Kuomintang and the Japanese, came into their own as policy guides for the whole country. Priorities were re-ordered: industry was to be geared to the needs of agriculture and developed not only in the cities but also and especially in the countryside, employing surplus rural labor and beginning the process of introducing the peasantry to modern technology. The absolute priority accorded to heavy industry in the Soviet model was abandoned, with the develop-

---

*The counterpart to this theory of the productive forces—as the Chinese have called it—is that the fatal flaw of capitalism was that it had finally become, in Marx's phrase, a fetter on the development of the forces of production, a proposition which seemed self-evident in the 1930s. Note that this theory had the effect of making analysis of other contradictions of capitalism unimportant and unnecessary. (One example which readily comes to mind in the nuclear age is that capitalism might *overdevelop* the forces of production in self-destructive ways without being able to provide any effective controls. Another is that in its unlimited urge to expand it might in effect destroy its own natural base and environment.)

ment of heavy industry also being integrated into a strategy which put agriculture (and the 80 percent of the people dependent on it) at the top of the nation's concerns. This meant that the "capital" needed to develop the Chinese economy was to come not from any pre-existing source of surplus—as both bourgeois economic theory and the Soviet orthodoxy of the period believed essential— but from a general increase in the productivity (agricultural and industrial alike) of the Chinese labor force. In this way the imposition of a special burden on any particular section of the population could be avoided and the whole issue of primitive socialist accumulation rendered irrelevant and meaningless. And politically this would permit the maintenance and even strengthening of the worker-peasant alliance, which in turn would make the build up of a specially repressive state apparatus as unnecessary as it would be irrational.

Carrying through this new strategy of development was by no means easy. It required a vast and historically unprecedented institutional innovation in the form of the agricultural communes; it suffered severe setbacks in the hard years of 1959–1962; and it finally got on track only with the introduction in 1962 and after of a Chinese version of the Green Revolution.[2] After that, however, it worked remarkably well: China became essentially self-sufficient in agricultural production; and industry developed, in terms of both rapidity and geographical distribution, in quite satisfactory fashion. It was thereby shown once and for all that the Soviet model, far from being an embodiment of the "laws" of socialism, was merely one possible path to economic development and in all probability one which is in irreconcilable contradiction with the requirements of a socialist transition toward communism. Never again, after the Chinese experience in the period 1955–1965, will a newly liberated country feel compelled to choose between the classical capitalist and Soviet roads to economic development.

This was the first momentous achievement of the Mao period. But it was not the only one. The Cultural Revolution was yet to come, and the issues involved, while closely related to the strategy of economic development, were also of a different order.

The basic problem can perhaps best be understood if set in the perspective of orthodox Soviet political theory of the 1930s.

According to this theory, the proletarian revolution overthrows capitalism and/or other forms of class society by abolishing private ownership of the means of production. The government which presides over this process and at the same time takes in hand the task of developing the forces of production is a dictatorship of the proletariat in the specific sense that it represses the old possessing classes and thwarts their inevitable counter-revolutionary efforts. Vis-à-vis the working class and its peasant allies, however, the revolutionary government is a democracy much more genuine than even the freest of bourgeois democracies. From these premises it follows that with the dying out of the old bourgeois and feudal ruling classes, the development of the forces of production, and the continuous elevation of the standard of living of the mass of the people, the class struggle will diminish in intensity and gradually disappear; and the state as a special apparatus of repression will, in the classical Marxian phrase, "wither away." To be sure, these processes will not be able to work their way through to completion as long as capitalism exists on an international scale and the world bourgeoisie continues to support the counterrevolutionary ambitions of the overthrown classes: during this period the state will continue to exist as a repressive apparatus against outside intervention. But this will not affect the basic tendencies at work as far as the internal structure and dynamics of the post-revolutionary society are concerned. Here democracy will flourish, and the path to a future transition to communism will be mapped out, subject only to the requirement of an adequate development of the forces of production.

The trouble with this theory of course was that it was in no way borne out by the experience of the Soviet Union. From the earliest days of the revolutionary government, repression was directed at large sections of the population, not only at the deposed exploiting classes; and this became an increasing, not a decreasing, characteristic of Soviet society with the passage of time. Responses to this situation were of several kinds: Orthodox Stalinists simply denied that there was any massive internal repression, their propaganda becoming more and more strident in proportion to its obvious belying of the facts. The other main reactions were those of the various brands of Trotskyists, all of whom were agreed that what was happening in the USSR was an aberration from, rather than a refutation of, the basic theory, and all of whom stressed the backwardness of traditional Russian society as the underlying cause. According to this view, a backward society inevitably inherits and/or breeds a large bureaucracy to perform economic and political managerial functions. Either this bureaucracy will be kept under the democratic control of the workers and their allies until, with the development of the productive forces, it is no longer necessary and can be dispensed with, or it will grab the levers of power and repress the masses, which is what happened in the Soviet Union under Stalin. At this point there was a division between those who, following Trotsky himself, believed that sooner or later a second—this time purely political—revolution would be necessary to restore power to the masses. Others, of whom Isaac Deutscher was perhaps the leading representative, took the position that after the death of Stalin, as the educational and cultural level of the Soviet peoples rose under the impact of the developing forces of production, a gradual process of democratization would set in which would eventually bring the Soviet Union into line with the theory sketched above.

It is important to recognize that none of what may be called these "aberration theories," no matter how scathingly critical of developments in the Soviet Union, had any place for the idea that the results of the October Revolution had been or were in the process of being negated. The bureaucracy was seen as an unavoidable excrescence on an otherwise healthy body politic, one which could and would be removed, either violently or peacefully, when the consequences of backwardness had been sufficiently overcome.*

However plausible this view may have seemed in the 1930s, or even two decades later, it certainly appears in a very different light today, sixty years after the October Revolution and more than a quarter of a century after World War II. The extreme

---

*A logical corollary, which however need not concern us in the present context, is that a post-revolutionary society in an already developed country would not be subject to the evils which had befallen the Soviet Union.

methods of repression in use under Stalin were abandoned after his death, but Deutscher's optimistic assumption that a gradual process of democratization had been initiated proved to be without foundation. And above all the notion that the combination of state ownership of the means of production plus rapid development of the forces of production would somehow open the socialist road to communism has turned out to be the grand illusion of the Marxism of the period of the Third International. The Soviet Union is now the world's second industrial power with a high level of popular education and a vast trained intelligentsia, and yet its working class has no access to political power, is barred from any form of self-organization, and probably has less influence on its conditions and methods of work than the working classes of the advanced European capitalist countries.

Evidently there was something radically wrong with the political theories of the Stalin period, including both those of the official Stalinists and those of their main opponents. The Soviet Union was neither a developing socialist democracy, modified only to the extent necessary to defend itself against external counterrevolutionary intervention, nor was it basically a healthy workers' state temporarily deflected from its natural course of development by the rule of an overweening bureaucracy. In reality it had become a social formation which was neither foreseen nor easily accounted for by any of the existing versions of Marxian theory. To illuminate this situation and lay at least the foundations for a more adequate Marxian theory of post-revolutionary society was the second great accomplishment of China under Mao's leadership.

Here, as in the case of the rejection of the Soviet model of economic development, it was practice which led the way and theory which lagged behind. "Learning from the Soviet Union," which was a cardinal principle in China in the first years after the takeover of power in 1949, naturally meant copying much in addition to the central strategy of economic development. Bureaucratic and elitist practices permeated all sectors of Chinese society, including the economy, government, and education. These were very much in the tradition of age-old Confucian habits of thought and action and hence were easily assimilated by those newly in authority. On the other hand, they were in sharp contrast to many of the ways of doing things that had evolved in the years of civil strife, resistance to Japanese invaders, and governance of large border regions in the 1930s and 1940s. Chinese Communism thus developed a kind of split personality, deeply rooted in the history of China as well as in its own history as a revolutionary movement. Both tendencies were of course represented in the ruling Communist Party, with Liu Shao-chi as the most prominent figure in the conservative or right-wing camp and Mao Tsetung holding the same position in the radical or left-wing camp. Not that this division was altogether new: in one form or another, indeed, it went back to the very beginnings of the party, but its full and fateful significance could only come to the fore after the seizure of power and the assumption of responsibility for the future course of the country as a whole.

This is not the place for a review of the history of what later came to be known as the "two-line struggle" in the period between 1949 and the Cultural Revolution. Suffice it to say that as long as the problem was one of overthrowing the old order and securely establishing the new, the differences remained in the background. But the more attention had to be focused on what the shape of the new order was to be, the more the differences came to the fore, with the Liuist tendency embracing the Soviet model and all that went with it, and the Maoists struggling to deepen the revolution and carry it forward from one stage to the next, always in the direction of greater equality and fuller participation by the masses in controlling and managing their own lives. The Maoists scored an important victory with the Great Leap Forward and the immediately following fall of Peng Teh-huai, but the opposition made a strong comeback in the "hard years," and the early 1960s witnessed the proliferation of elitist tendencies in both economics and politics.

This was the setting for the Cultural Revolution. It originated in a revolt of university students—comparable to similar movements in the West—against exaggerated forms of elitism deeply rooted in Chinese tradition, and from there it spread to the schools and other sectors of the younger generation. Mao, whose dominance in the country's leadership had suffered a partial eclipse in the rightward movement of the early 1960s, saw in this uprising of the youth his opportunity to regain the initiative for the left. Using such slogans as "It Is Justified to Rebel" and "Bombard the Headquarters," he embarked the country on a three-year voyage through stormy seas and rocky shoals, coming perilously close to shipwreck on more than one occasion. The schools and universities were closed while students roamed the country with the revolutionary message; many leaders were dismissed and disgraced; party committees were disbanded and replaced by new "revolutionary committees"; and the People's Liberation Army had to be called upon in numerous situations to prevent factional struggles from degenerating into civil war. And all the while the post-Great Leap move to the right was being reversed, and the initiative in matters of economic and social policy was passing into the hands of those who stood for propelling the revolution forward in the direction of greater equality and greater mass participation.

It would take someone far more knowledgeable than myself to trace the impact of these tremendous social upheavals in the realm of theory. I shall therefore focus entirely on one aspect and one outcome which seem to me to have fundamentally and definitively transformed Marxian political theory as it had taken shape in the period of the Third International.

Among the Chinese themselves there has never been any doubt that all the struggles which have taken place since 1949 have been in one way or another manifestations of class struggle which, since the appearance of the *Communist Manifesto,* has been seen by Marxists as the motor force of historical change since the period of primitive communism. But precisely what is meant by class struggle in a modern post-revolutionary society has never to this day been satisfactorily analyzed or explained. There are three strands of thought here which need to be clearly distinguished.

(1) The overthrow of a bourgeois and/or feudal regime does not do away with the old exploiting classes. These will of course strive by every available means to defeat their conquerors and to return to power. In the course of doing so they will wage fierce class struggles which can be expected to continue until the old exploiting classes have died out. All Marxists, whatever their

differences, agree that in this sense class struggle is an inevitable feature of post-revolutionary society.

(2) The ideas, values, and habits of thought and behavior of the old ruling classes—which, Marx insisted, have always been the ruling ideas of a society—do not die out with their progenitors. They are deeply imbedded in all strata of society, and this is especially true of the educated elements which naturally play a prominent role in revolutionary leaderships. The struggle to get rid of this inherited and necessarily counterrevolutionary mental baggage is also in a very real sense a class struggle, though Marxists have not always identified it as such.

(3) The third strand is the most complicated and the least understood. Running a post-revolutionary society requires administrators, managers, technicians, experts of various kinds; and, compared to ordinary workers and peasants, the people occupying these positions have higher incomes and dispose over substantial perquisites and power. Regardless of class origin or degree of subjection to the dominance of old ideas, those who enjoy such privileged positions soon develop a vested interest in maintaining them and seek, consciously or unconsciously, to pass them along to their children. (To a considerable extent this inter-generational transmittal of privileged position happens anyway, since children of favored households have an important head-start in school which, on the average, means that the chances of following in their parents' footsteps are better than those of their less-favored classmates.) All of this of course has long been known to sociologists, and (so far as I know) has never been denied by Marxists. But given the premises of the orthodox political theory of the Stalin period, these questions of relative power and privilege were treated as part of the problematic of bureaucracy rather than class, classes being entirely defined and circumscribed by the property system. According to this theory, in a socialist setting the very existence of a bureaucracy, whatever its undesirable qualities and tendencies, was a temporary and transitional phenomenon. With the inevitable development of the productive forces (un-leashed by the abolition of private property in the means of production), the conditions necessitating a bureaucracy would gradually disappear and the stratum itself would follow in due

course. In the meantime—and this is a crucially important point—the struggle against bureaucracy would take the form of measures to control excesses and inculcate in bureaucrats a greater sense of social responsibility. The argument in a nutshell is that elites are inevitable for a long time to come (until they more or less automatically disappear), but they ought to be well-behaved elites. On the other hand, if one takes the position that the managerial stratum is not a bureaucracy in this sense but rather an incipient ruling (and exploiting) class, then the struggle against it must be a class struggle in the full sense of the term, with the ultimate objective not of controlling it and making it more socially responsible but of eliminating it altogether and achieving a genuinely classless society. This in turn implies the belief that workers and peasants, through prolonged struggle lasting a whole historical epoch but beginning immediately, can themselves master and assume responsibility for the functions which are carried out by the privileged managers and bureaucrats in the first post-revolutionary phase.

Against this background, the thesis which I am concerned to uphold can be briefly stated. In the Chinese political discussions, debates, and polemics of the 1950s and 1960s, the meaning of the term "class struggle" gradually shifted from almost exclusive emphasis on the first sense sketched above to a combination of the second and third senses, with the third having acquired clear predominance by the end of the Cultural Revolution. In other words the class enemy, which the workers and their allies were being exhorted to struggle against, started out being the old ruling classes, increasingly became elites (and others as well) still dominated by the ideas, values, etc., of the old ruling classes, and ended up being a "new bourgeoisie" produced (and incessantly reproduced) by the social formation which had emerged from the revolution itself.

That this last conception of classes and class struggle in post-revolutionary society is as applicable to the Soviet Union as to China is obvious: indeed, the evidence and reasoning to support it came at least as much from Soviet as from Chinese experience. It is also obvious that its implications for the political theory inherited by China from the Soviet Union are devastating. The notion that abolition of private property in the means of production ushers in an essentially classless society which, given a sufficient development of the forces of production, will evolve in a harmonious way toward communism—this notion is exploded once and for all. In its place we have a conception of socialism as a class-divided society like all that have preceded it, and one which has the potential to move forward or backward depending on the fortunes of a class struggle through which alone the human race can aspire to leave behind the horrors and miseries of the past and lay the foundations for a future worthy of its capabilities.

Many will find this a discouraging conclusion. Revolution, they firmly believed, would mark a decisive turning point, after which progress, however slow and painful, could only be in the direction of the higher stage of communism of which Marx wrote in *The Critique of the Gotha Program*. What had to be overcome was the terrible heritage of the past, not the inherent contradictions of the new society. The experience of the Mao period shattered this optimistic illusion. Post-revolutionary society contains not only contradictions inherited from millennia of class-riven society, but it produces and reproduces its own contradictions. The revolution provides no final solutions. It only opens the possibility of moving forward *in the direction* of eliminating classes. But the existence of this as a possibility implies its opposite, the possibility of moving backward toward the re-entrenchment of an exploiting class based not on private property in the means of production but on control of an all-encompassing repressive state apparatus.

According to the theory developed in the Mao period, this is precisely what actually happened in the Soviet Union. Would it also happen in China after Mao? That it might is inherent in the theory itself. Whether it will can only depend on the still unknown future course of a class struggle, the meaning and importance of which must now be recognized and pondered by all who seek to understand the historical period in which we live.

(February 1977)

7
CHARLES BETTELHEIM
ON REVOLUTION FROM ABOVE:
THE USSR IN THE 1920s

The great Russian Revolution of 1917 is known as the October Revolution because it was in the month of October (by the old Russian calendar) that the Bolsheviks seized power in Petrograd and, soon after, in other major cities. The designation of course is an oversimplification. What happened in the cities was only one aspect of the revolution; the other aspect, far larger in scale and sweep, took place in the countryside with the seizure of the large estates and their division into millions of small holdings. This was one of history's greatest agrarian uprisings up to that time, and it sealed the fate of the old order in the Tsarist empire. The Bolsheviks, quite literally, were not represented in the country-side: theirs was an urban working-class movement. And yet they were able to hold onto power at the center and to organize and lead a victorious struggle against the forces of counterrevolution, domestic and foreign alike, which fought tooth-and-nail for four long and bitter years to restore the status quo ante. The explanation of this apparent paradox is simple. The peasants knew that defeat for the Bolsheviks would mean the return to power of their age-old exploiters and oppressors. Only by waging a common struggle against a common foe could the gains of 1917–1918 be defended and secured.

This was the origin of the worker-peasant alliance in the Russian Revolution. It was imposed on both sides by the imperatives of a life-and-death struggle. Though wholeheartedly welcomed by the Bolsheviks, it was not a policy which they could claim to have planned or deliberately put into operation. For the peasants it was strictly a matter of self-interest in the most obvious and immediate sense.

With the end of the Civil War and the defeat of the counter-revolution, all this changed. The Bolsheviks were a Marxist party, more consciously and determinedly so than any other in the world up to that time. Their aim was to transform Tsarist Russia into a socialist society which, as Lenin made clear in many of his writings, they interpreted in a literal (and radical) Marxian sense. This meant, among other things, gradually assimilating the peasantry into the working class—i.e., turning tens of millions of individualistic smallholders into mutually supporting, socially conscious farmworkers—as a step on the way to eliminating classes altogether. And while every Marxist would contend that this was and is in the long-term best interests of the peasants themselves, few if any believed that it was what the peasants perceived to be in their interest or set themselves as a goal. What the peasants wanted in Russia in the early 1920s was the creation of conditions under which they could enjoy the fruits of the gains achieved in the revolution and defended in the civil war; and this meant essentially no rents, minimal taxes, and the ability to sell and buy as needed to sustain themselves and their petty enterprises.

In these circumstances the Bolsheviks were confronted with two basic problems. The first was short term and of the greatest urgency. The civil war had imposed enormous burdens on the peasantry—conscription of manpower for the Red armies, requisitioning of draft animals and foodstuffs, etc. In the last phases of the fighting, famine was spreading to many parts of the country and peasant unrest was rapidly rising and taking increasingly menacing forms. The worker-peasant alliance was visibly disintegrating; the country was sinking into a state of ungovernable chaos. How could this disastrous course be checked and reversed? How could the basis of the worker-peasant alliance, so crucial to the very functioning of a viable social order, be restored? The second problem was long run but, from the Bolshevik point of view, no less important on that account. How, in the conditions prevailing in Russia after seven years of war and revolution with all their destructive consequences, could the transformation of the peasantry called for by Marxist theory be set in motion? How could the worker-peasant alliance be not only restored but turned into a *process* of ultimate merger?

There were two ways of viewing these issues. The first saw them as entirely separate and distinct. The economy, and particularly its overwhelmingly preponderant agricultural component, would have to be restored to something like its prewar condition before any meaningful long-term strategy could be devised. This could be achieved only by far-reaching concessions to the peasantry— restoration of a stable currency, establishment of free markets in the countryside, an end to requisitioning and the substitution of a predictable and equitable system of taxation, etc. Given these conditions, agriculture would recover and the peasants would see that the Soviet government both respected their interests and at the same time offered them the best guarantee against the return of the landlords. The worker-peasant alliance would thus be restored. The transformation of the peasantry, while not given up as an ultimate objective, would have to be put off until some time in the future.

The second way of viewing the two basic problems facing the Bolsheviks at the end of the civil war was to see them as inextricably intertwined. The necessary recovery of agriculture would indeed require far-reaching concessions to the peasantry, but these should be combined (i.e., initiated and carried out simultaneously) with policies designed to begin their transformation. This could take place only via the development of cooperatives among the poor and middle peasants. This in turn would have to be voluntary on the part of the peasants, since any use of coercion would be damaging to the prospects of the worker-peasant alliance and hence self-defeating. What was required of the Soviet government was therefore policies aimed on the one hand at providing the poor and middle peasants with material assistance and incentives which would convince them that traveling the cooperative route was in their own best interests, and on the other hand at remolding the attitudes and outlook of the peasants from those of isolated petty producers to those of socially conscious members of the whole society. The introduction of these policies, however, should not be postponed to some indefinite time in the future but should take place as soon as possible; otherwise new class relations in the countryside might develop and become frozen into a mold which would stubbornly resist any further efforts at change.

The New Economic Policy (NEP) was inaugurated in 1921.* How did it respond to these basic problems? Was it essentially a temporary "retreat," a package of concessions to the peasantry (and other nonproletarian segments of the population), designed to get the economy back on its feet again but to be withdrawn at the earliest opportunity? Or was it rather an attempt to implement the second view sketched above, i.e., to restore the worker-peasant alliance while at the same time setting in motion the process of transforming the peasantry along the lines which Marxian theory held to be essential to a successful transition to socialism?

This is approximately where the second volume of *Class Struggles in the USSR,* Charles Bettelheim's large-scale reinterpretive study of Soviet history, begins.[1] Its subject is the worker-peasant alliance and its relation to the NEP. Let me attempt to sketch the basic framework of Bettelheim's argument.

There were many people in Russia at the time, both in and out of the Bolshevik Party, who saw the NEP only as a set of concessions to get the economy going again, a tactical maneuver to be abandoned when it had accomplished its purpose. (Later on, this interpretation became even more widespread: when I was introduced to Marxism some ten years later, I don't remember its even being questioned.) As Bettelheim clearly shows, however, this was emphatically not Lenin's view nor officially that of the party of which he was then the undisputed political and ideological leader. Already at the Eleventh Party Congress (April 1922) Lenin proclaimed an end to the "retreat" phase of the NEP but not an end to the NEP itself. From then on the NEP was to be the vehicle for a new advance. "The main thing now," Bettelheim quotes Lenin as saying (p. 24), "is to advance as an immeasurably wider and larger mass, and *only together with the peasantry,* proving to them by deeds, in practice, by experience, that we are learning

---

*The NEP comprised a complex of measures. Apart from those affecting the peasantry, small traders and producers (who became known as Nepmen) were permitted to operate, limited concessions to foreign investors were authorized, etc. Here we are concerned only with the NEP as the foundation of the country's agricultural policy.

and that we shall learn *to assist them, to lead them forward.*" Thus for Lenin the NEP, properly understood, was in no sense a *tactical maneuver* but rather the crucial element of the Bolsheviks' long-term *strategy* for achieving socialism.

For the next few years, until 1926, the NEP worked quite well as an economic recovery program. Production, both agricultural and industrial, bounced back to roughly prewar levels, living standards improved, and the threat to Soviet power subsided. But despite reiterated declarations by the party of adherence to the Leninist concept of the NEP, very little was attempted and even less accomplished toward transforming productive (and hence also social) relations in the countryside. And after 1926 it soon became apparent that the route being traveled was in reality a blind alley. Agricultural production stagnated; worse yet, the marketed surplus of grain purchased from the peasants by the state and cooperative trading organizations suffered serious setbacks, threatening the food supply of the cities and under-mining the country's export capability, and hence also its ability to import much-needed industrial products. The immediate causes of this situation were clear enough. On the one hand, the peasants, freed of onerous rent payments to landlords, were eating more (and feeding more to their livestock); on the other hand, a con-tinuing and even worsening shortage of manufactured goods acted in two ways to hold down the supply of agricultural products offered for sale: lack of much-needed tools, implements, and materials stymied efforts to increase production, and inability to buy consumer goods reduced the peasants' incentive to sell what they did manage to produce.

This crisis of the marketed surplus was, not surprisingly, gen-erally interpreted as a crisis of the NEP. We shall return presently to the question of whether this is a correct evaluation; here it is enough to point out that it initiated a series of events which led in the short space of two years to the "great change" (Stalin's term) of 1928–1929 and the total abandonment of the NEP—though, as Bettelheim reminds us, the term itself lingered on in official party pronouncements into the 1930s. The heart of the matter was the adoption by the party of "exceptional measures" (in effect, forced requisitioning) to increase the collection of grain to meet the needs of the cities and of export. Intended to be temporary, these measures actually had the effect of making their continuation increasingly essential. The peasants reacted negatively. Production faltered, the marketed surplus suffered further reverses, and even more stringent "exceptional measures" became necessary. A vicious cycle had been set in motion, and the leadership could see no way to break out of it except through a crash program of collectivization combined with accelerated industrialization. Here, as quoted by Bettelheim (p. 589), is the way the official party history (published ten years later) summed up the situation:

> All the signs pointed to the danger of a further decline in the amount of marketable grain. . . . There was a crisis in grain farming which was bound to be followed by a crisis in livestock farming. The only escape from this predicament was a change to large-scale farming which would permit the use of tractors and agricultural machines . . . , to take the course of amalgamating the small peasant holdings into large *socialist* farms, collective farms, which would be able to use tractors and other modern machines for a rapid advancement of grain farming and a rapid increase in the marketable surplus of grain.

An almost identical interpretation was put forward a quarter of a century later by the Soviet historian Yakovtsevsky. Again as quoted by Bettelheim (p. 590):

> The lagging of agriculture behind industry . . . showed that the impulse to development given to agriculture by the October Revolution had, in the main, been exhausted. The old social basis—small-scale individual peasant farming—could no longer be the source of further development for agriculture. An urgent necessity had been created for agricultural production to move over on to the rails of large-scale collective farming.

This purely economic interpretation of the reasons for the "great change" was widely supplemented by a political one which related the troubles of the marketed surplus to the alleged growth in the power of the kulaks (rich peasants) in the countryside.*

---

*Sometimes the term kulak is used in a narrower sense to designate those rich peasants who hire the labor of others. Like many other writers, however, Bettelheim uses the term kulak and rich peasant interchangeably.

According to this view, the kulaks were largely responsible for withholding grain from market as a form of struggle against the Soviet government. Failure to break this growing kulak power would ultimately result in the triumph of counterrevolution and the restoration of capitalism in Russia. Massive collectivization would therefore simultaneously solve the biggest and most urgent problems confronting the Soviet government: guaranteeing an adequate supply of grain to the state and breaking the back of the counterrevolution.

It is hardly an exaggeration to say that Bettelheim's entire volume is devoted to the refutation of these interlinked explanations of the crisis and "great change" of 1928–1929, and one can only admire the way he has carried out the task, examining the central issues from all relevant points of view and marshaling his evidence from both documentary and secondary sources with extraordinary care and skill. Under the circumstances it would be presumptuous to attempt a rounded presentation of the case he builds up; we must be content to select and emphasize a number of highlights as a preliminary to raising certain issues which, in my opinion, deserve further thought and research.

First, let us dispose of the kulak argument. Drawing extensively on recent monographic studies,[2] Bettelheim convincingly shows that this was never well founded and that to the extent that the power of the kulaks was increasing in the late 1920s, the reason was not their inherent economic strength but rather the growing hostility of the middle and even some of the poor peasants to the policies of the Soviet government. The division of the great estates in the October Revolution left Soviet agriculture with a relatively egalitarian structure, and the dominant trend during the first five years of the NEP was a proportional *increase* in the number of middle peasants, and *decline* in the number of poor peasants, some of whom were proletarianized while others achieved the status of middle peasants. The class of rich peasants also expanded but only very moderately. Bettelheim cites reliable Soviet sources to the effect that in 1926–1927 the peasantry was divided as follows: poor—29.4 percent; middle—67.5 percent; rich—3.1 percent. (p. 88) The contribution of the rich peasants to the marketed surplus was naturally larger, but still only 11.8

percent of the total, while the poor and middle peasants together delivered the remainder, i.e., over 88 percent. This is not to argue that the kulaks were unimportant, but it should be enough to dispose of the claim, first advanced by the opposition within the party and later taken up by the leadership, that the kulaks were at the heart of the difficulties besetting the Soviet Union in the mid-1920s.*

What about the general economic argument that the potentialities of the agricultural setup created by the upheavals of 1917–1918 were exhausted and that further progress of agriculture—and hence also for Soviet society as a whole—depended on the earliest possible realization of collectivization and mechanization? Bettelheim's answer to this can be divided into two parts. First, the potentialities of Soviet agriculture as it existed in the mid-1920s had by no means been exhausted. He presents persuasive evidence to show that a significant proportion of peasant holdings was not being cultivated, not because of any shortage of humanpower (there was much under- and unemployment in the countryside) but because of a lack of (mostly simple) tools and implements, seeds, etc.[3] Second, given this situation, there was no urgent need for a drastic changeover to collectivization and mechanization. What was required was rather a policy of providing the peasantry with the wherewithal to expand production on the existing basis. To be sure, such a policy would necessarily be many-sided. It would have to include at a minimum an appropriate orientation of industrial production both in urban state enterprises and in village handicrafts, and the provision of effective assistance (especially in the form of credit facilities from state and cooperative sources) for poor and middle peasants.

But, you may ask, isn't this precisely what the NEP was supposed to be all about? Didn't Lenin insist (see the quotation above) that the only way to socialism in the USSR was through helping the peasants and in doing so convincing them that their own best interests would be served by working together rather than sepa-

*Their power in the countryside was based not so much on their control of a grain surplus as on their role as moneylenders and local power-wielders. Breaking this power was of course essential to a socialist solution of the agrarian problem, but the way adopted in 1928–1929 was not the only possible one.

rately?* And if the answer to these questions is yes, as it surely must be, then the next question that arises is: What went wrong? And here we come to the heart of Bettelheim's whole argument.

This particular crisis (there were of course others besetting Soviet society in the mid-1920s) was not a crisis of the NEP but rather a crisis arising from failure to adhere to and carry through the NEP. And this failure had its origin not in agriculture but in the industrialization policies of the Soviet government. These policies, beginning around 1926 (i.e., long before the "great change"), aimed not only at an accelerated *rate* of industrialization, but also at a particular *kind* of industrialization—large scale, urban, using the most advanced technology available. Both aspects (rate and kind) had far-reaching implications for Soviet society as a whole, and particularly for agriculture. First, there was the problem of financing a more rapid pace of industrialization, and in the situation then existing this involved budgetary deficits and inflating the money supply, with consequent disruption of the price structure, shortages, bottlenecks, etc. This alone would have been enough to exacerbate the problems of provisioning the countryside. But the kind of industrialization favored by the government made matters worse. Concentration on modern large-scale urban industry was one side of the coin; the other side was neglecting or actually cutting back on all other kinds of industrial production, including not only production of consumer goods but also production of relatively simple types of means of production which are so crucially important to the functioning of peasant agriculture (hoes, shovels, carts, axes, hammers, saws, wire, nails, etc., etc.).

---

*Bettelheim, basing himself on the work of Sigrid Grosskopf cited in n. 2, shows that there was widespread receptivity to cooperative forms of organization during the NEP but that most of what was accomplished was done by the peasants themselves with little or no help from the government. In summary he says: "True, from the standpoint of the general structure of Soviet agriculture, the existence of these various types of organization of the poor and middle peasants did not alter the massive predominance of individual peasant farming. Nevertheless, their existence, by the very multiplicity of the forms they assumed and the liveliness and depth of the tendencies they manifested (despite the absence of systematic aid from the Soviet government and the hostility of the rich peasants), shows how great were the possibilities for transition to a socialist organization of agriculture." (p. 101)

The latter had traditionally been the province of a great variety of village handicrafts which now found themselves starved of needed inputs or in some cases actually shut down as supposedly harmful competitors of the new "socialist" enterprises. To understand the full meaning of this situation, it is necessary to add that by 1926 the stock of means of production in the hands of the peasants had by no means been restored to the 1913 level and that the strong recovery of production in the early years of the NEP was first and foremost a tribute to the hard work and resourcefulness of men and women who were now working for themselves and no longer for a parasitic landlord class. But the gains that could be achieved in this way obviously had their limits, and the stagnation of production which set in after 1926 demonstrated that these limits had been reached. For the further progress of agricultural production what was now needed was a more ample supply of the tools, implements, and materials that would make possible a continued increase in the productivity of the peasants' labor.

The conclusion of this line of reasoning is thus not at all the one drawn from the events of the time by the Soviet leadership and subsequently elevated to the status of axiomatic truth by the party and its official and unofficial spokesmen. It is simply not true that (in the words of Yakovtsevsky quoted above) "the old social basis—small-scale individual peasant farming—could no longer be the source of further development for agriculture." It might have been said, quite correctly, that small individual cultivation did not provide a foundation for the *socialist* development of agriculture. But that was true from the beginning and was fully understood by all Marxists: there was never any dispute about the eventual necessity of transcending small individual cultivation. The "only" question was how to do it.

As we have seen, the NEP was intended to provide the answer. Its nonapplication by the Soviet leadership led to an impasse; and the attempt to escape from the impasse impelled Stalin onto a course which was in important respects the very opposite of that championed by Lenin, who believed that the worker-peasant alliance—which to him was the essence and the *sina qua non* of the dictatorship of the proletariat—required faithful adherence to the principle of noncoercion vis-à-vis the peasants. As Lenin might have predicted, therefore, the forced requisitioning of 1927–1928 followed by the forced collectivization campaign of 1928–1929 effectively destroyed the alliance and barred the road to the socialist development of Soviet society.*

Before we ask *why* the NEP was never properly implemented and *why* an industrialization policy which negated the NEP was adopted in 1926, a few words seem called for concerning the real (historical) meaning of the forced collectivization of Soviet agriculture. This is the more important because, though I have no doubt that he is clear enough in his own mind, Bettelheim does not explicitly spell out what is at issue in terms likely to clarify the matter for all his readers. Recall first that pre-revolutionary Russian society rested squarely on the exploitation of the peasantry. (The proletariat was of course also exploited, but it was small and its contribution to the country's surplus product still relatively modest.) The revolution destroyed the set of social relations which made this exploitation of the peasantry possible. The peasants now controlled their own surplus product, consumed much more of it directly, and exchanged for manufactured goods (means of production and consumer goods) only so much of the total as seemed to them at any given time to be in their own best interest. As long as both agriculture and industry were recovering from the disastrous declines of the civil war period, this arrangement worked passably well. But with the end of this phase it showed itself to be an unstable and unreliable foundation for the new Soviet society. Either arrangements would be devised which would convince the peasants that it was in fact in their best interest to bring enough of their surplus product to market to underpin the system and permit its expansion (*and* make it possible for them to do so), or it would be necessary to reestablish in one form or another a set of social relations which would deprive the peasantry of control over its surplus product and subject it once again to a regime of exploitation by an alien power.

---

*This is my own interpretation. In the volume under review Bettelheim says only that the worker-peasant alliance was "seriously weakened" (*gravement affaiblie*); and he expresses no opinion about whether there were still possibilities for the Soviet Union to advance in the direction of socialism. We shall have to wait for his third volume to discover his views on this subject.

In theory of course—official Bolshevik theory—this was neither the intent nor the effect of the "great change." Collectivization combined with mechanization (made possible by accelerated industrialization) was supposed to initiate a rapid increase in agricultural output, and this in turn would enable the peasantry to raise its standard of living and at the same time deliver the required amounts of grain to the state. But it didn't work that way, and history attaches little credit to good intentions. In fact Soviet agricultural output not only declined in the short run but entered into a long-run period of stagnation and crises from which it has still, a half century later, not fully recovered. And yet, looked at from another point of view, the "revolution from above" launched in 1928–1929 (the term was used approvingly by the Bolsheviks themselves) cannot be judged a failure. The new production relations in the countryside (the collective farms crucially buttressed by the state-owned and state-run machine-tractor stations) placed the peasantry back in a straitjacket very different in some respects from, and yet similar in others to, that in which they had been confined before the revolution. Only now it was not a rent-collecting landlord class which was the immediate appropriator of their surplus product, but a tribute-gathering central state.*

We come now to the question as to why events took the course they did in the mid-1920s—why the original conception of the NEP was not carried out and why an industrialization policy was adopted which effectively foreclosed the possibility of a return to that development strategy. Bettelheim's answer, if I understand him correctly, stressed two points. First, the Bolsheviks being an urban working-class party did not really understand the needs or the potentialities of the peasantry. As a result, despite paying lip-service to Lenin's conception of the NEP and its relation to the peasants, they lacked either the knowledge or the will (or both) to

---

*It is interesting that Stalin himself, in 1928 and 1929, spoke of the necessity of imposing "something in the nature of a 'tribute'" on the peasantry to support the country's industrialization. (Bettelheim, pp. 401, 428) In this he was advancing essentially the same idea as the one he had rejected when it was put forward earlier by the Trotskyist opposition, and especially championed by Preobrazhensky, under the label of "primitive socialist accumulation."

implement it and in effect treated it not as a strategy for achieving socialism but as a tactical retreat to be abandoned as soon as conditions would permit. Second, Bolshevik ideology (i.e., their brand of Marxism) included a deep distrust of the peasantry and a strong predeliction for the most rapid possible expansion of modern large-scale industry, perceived as the best way to promote the development of the forces of production and increase the size and social weight of the proletariat. These two facts, reinforcing each other, pushed the Soviet economy into the impasse of 1927–1928 and frustrated all escape efforts short of the drastic "revolution from above" launched in 1928–1929.

In my view this explanation is entirely valid as far as it goes. The Bolsheviks' lack of knowledge and experience with respect to agriculture was indeed profound (how could it be otherwise?),* and the Marxism of the period—not only the Bolshevik version—undoubtedly had a strong tendency to identify socialism with large-scale machine industry and its associated working class. Moreover in the Russian case this bias in favor of large-scale machine industry was much reinforced by the Bolsheviks' own history: their strongholds from the beginning had been the relatively new factories of European Russia and in particular those implanted by foreign capital, such as the Putilov works in Petrograd, which were among the largest and most advanced in the world at the time.†

At the same time it will hardly escape the reader's attention that this way of explaining the course of events in the mid-1920s

---

*In this respect the contrast with the situation in China after 1949 could hardly be sharper, and goes far toward accounting for the divergent courses taken by the Russian and Chinese revolutions. The Chinese Communist Party had long years of experience in governing rural border areas, and a large proportion of its cadres were themselves peasants.

†This ideological preference for large-scale production has remained and has been reflected in Soviet economic practice at all stages of development. As Harry Magdoff has pointed out, "Almost 62 percent of industrial employment in the Soviet Union is in large-size plants; fewer than 30 percent of U.S. plants have more than one thousand employees." And the difference is especially marked in the machine-tool and metal-working enterprises: "The average-size plant of these enterprises in the USSR, as measured by the number of employees, is thirty-five times that of the United States, as compared with twelve times for all industries."[4]

relates to the history and inherited ideology of the Bolsheviks rather than to current developments in the realms of social relations, political power, and ideology. I hasten to add that the problem is not that Bettelheim neglects these subjects or fails to provide valuable material on what was happening with respect to them. The problem, I believe, is that he does not integrate this material into his basic explanatory schema and in the process develop the interconnections and implications in a way which will bring the lessons of this crucial segment of Soviet history into sharp focus for his readers. In what follows I obviously have no such ambitious intentions: I want merely to make a few suggestions and raise a few questions.

Bettelheim, as the title of his opus indicates, is fully aware of the need to connect major developments to class struggles. And yet with respect to the problem under consideration I do not think he succeeds in showing what this connection really was. The reason, I believe, is that his analysis makes certain implicit assumptions which are retained throughout, despite the fact that in the course of the analysis much material is introduced (in both volumes published to date) that contradicts these assumptions.

The assumptions, reduced to barest essentials, are: (1) that the chief actors on the stage of Soviet history during the 1920s were on the one hand the proletariat and its vanguard party which was in control of state power, and on the other hand the peasantry and its poor, middle, and rich subdivisions; (2) that the party, and hence the "Soviet power" (a term frequently used by Bettelheim), attempted to implement its traditional principles but operated under severe handicaps (faulty knowledge, lack of experience, inappropriate ideology); and (3) that the combination of these circumstances resulted in ineffective and often counterproductive policies, numerous "errors" (also a concept much used by Bettelheim), and ultimate failure.

Like all such abstract schemas, this one could at best be no more than an approximate representation of reality. In the rapidly changing conditions prevailing in the Soviet Union (as well as in the rest of the world) during the 1920s, however, it is doubtful if this schema or any other that might be devised could attain to even such a degree of reliability. And it is surely one of the great merits of Bettelheim's work that he provides all the evidence and insights needed to understand why this should be so.

First, the proletariat. It was decimated and dispersed during the civil war; its best and most experienced militants were either killed or absorbed into the administration of governmental and economic affairs. Later on, with economic recovery and the initiation of ambitious industrialization programs, it was reconstituted on a new basis and in conditions very unlike those of the late nineteenth and early twentieth centuries. The assumption that the "proletariat" or the "working class" are terms which stand for essentially the same social entity with the same aspirations and capabilities during this whole period of turmoil and upheaval is bound to be seriously misleading.

Second, the party. It started as the vanguard of the proletariat, but its fulfillment of this role became more and more ambiguous as time went by. The leadership core of "old Bolsheviks" remained relatively intact for a long time, but its social base as well as the class composition of the membership changed, as did the functions it was called on to perform. With both the proletariat and the party in a state of flux, the question is not whether the party ceased to be the vanguard of the proletariat but whether in that particular historical setting the concept itself any longer had a clear meaning.

Third, the "Soviet power." The party continued to occupy all the leading positions in the Soviet government, but to occupy leading positions is one thing and really to control state power is another. Bettelheim showed at length in the first volume of *Class Struggles* that already in Lenin's lifetime the state apparatus was staffed by elements predominantly hostile to socialism and the Bolshevik revolution. Under these circumstances the link between the formulation and execution of policies was at best uncertain and at worst nonexistent. One consequence is that what from one point of view may appear to be the result of "errors" from another point of view can be seen to have been caused by the intent or neglect of those responsible for executing official policies.

Fourth—and here I think we come to the crux of the matter— the class structure, or at any rate the ensemble of social forces determining the course of events, was undergoing fundamental alterations during the years of the NEP. Bettelheim is naturally well aware of this. In the foreword to the first volume he tells us (and of course I agree) that the Soviet Union today is a society with a new ruling class ("state bourgeoisie"), and later on in that volume he traces the beginnings of this phenomenon back to the years immediately following the October Revolution. In the volume here under consideration he does not stress this theme (presumably that will come in the volume or volumes dealing with the 1930s and after), but neither does he entirely neglect it.[5] This class-in-the-process-of-becoming had its existence in the state apparatus, in the party, and of course in the management of the economic enterprises in the state sector. Its membership came from diverse social backgrounds, it had common interests but was not fully conscious of them or how to pursue them, it lacked traditions and had no ideology of its own. It was, in short, far from having attained the status of a full-fledged class, let alone that of a ruling class. Nevertheless, it already had important class-like characteristics and I believe played an essentially class role in the history of the period.

What makes this so important in the present context is that the focus of this "class" role was precisely in the area to which Bettelheim assigns decisive importance in explaining the crisis of the mid-1920s and the end of the NEP, i.e., the area of industrial policy. The nascent state bourgeoisie had every interest in promoting the development of the state sector, and within the state sector that of large-scale modern forms of technology and organization. It therefore reinforced and made full use of all the biases and tendencies which the Bolsheviks had inherited from their own past. Viewed in this way, these biases and tendencies can be recognized not only as causative factors operating through the old Bolsheviks in leading positions, but also as the expression of the very real and active interests of a social stratum which was in any case rapidly expanding its power and influence.

If space permitted, this line of reasoning could be developed further and I believe with useful results. But in closing a brief comment will have to suffice. If the industrial policy initiated in 1926—favoring large-scale modern enterprises, starving village and rural handicrafts—reflected a sort of alliance between the old

Bolsheviks and the nascent state bourgeoisie, the consequences of this policy forced them into even closer association. The need to collect "tribute" from the peasantry placed them in joint opposition to by far the largest segment of the population. The effort to get out of this bind then drove them further along the same path. Forced collectivization and greatly accelerated industrialization seemed to offer the only way out, but at the same time it exacerbated the antagonism between the peasantry on the one hand and the state and industry on the other. For a while a rapidly expanding working class appeared to offer a more solid base for the party leadership, but the prospect was short lived. The surplus which could be squeezed out of the peasantry was too little to sustain the projected rate of industrialization, and it soon became necessary to add the working class itself to the sources of tribute. This left the party leadership with only the rising state bourgeoisie as a social base, and gave the latter the opportunity to infiltrate the party, gradually taking it over as its own instrument of rule and adapting its ideology, by now a strongly economistic form of Marxism, to the needs of the new situation.

Too simple, to be sure. But I believe this does indicate how one can go about the task of systematically relating developments in the Soviet Union in the 1920s (and after) to very concrete ongoing class struggles (or emerging class struggles) and not simply to class forces which had their roots in an earlier history.

(October 1977)

8
IS THERE A RULING CLASS IN THE USSR?

The answers most frequently given to this question can be divided into two major categories, each of which includes a number of variants. The first holds that there is indeed a ruling class in the USSR, but does not agree as to its nature and attributes. Some say it is a capitalist class, basically like the ruling classes in the developed capitalist countries though differing from them in relatively minor respects and degrees; others maintain that there is a ruling class but that it is of a new type, differing in essentials from hitherto existing ruling classes. The second major category of answers holds that there is no ruling *class* in the USSR, arguing instead that state power is in the hands of a "bureaucracy," but once again there is no consensus as to the meaning of the term.

I shall argue in favor of the thesis that there is a ruling class in the USSR and that it is of a new type. I shall proceed by way of an examination of the original and best known of the bureaucracy theories, that of Trotsky and his followers.[1] I must immediately add, however, that what follows is no more than a preliminary to a serious analysis of the whole "problematic" of the Soviet ruling class. That will have to wait for another occasion. But first it is necessary to be clear about the *existence* of such a class, and I think this can be most usefully demonstrated by a critique of the theory, dating back to the early days of the Soviet state, that it does not exist and could not exist without the prior restoration of private property in the means of production.

Underlying the Trotskyist theory is a version of the Marxist theory of the state which was widely accepted at the time of the Russian Revolution and indeed may be considered a staple element of Bolshevik doctrine then and later. Schematically, this version of the Marxist theory posits a society with a well-developed class structure. Classes are distinguished by their differing relations to the means of production and defined by a property system which gives to the society a legally sanctioned and enforceable structure. The primary and overriding function of the state is to maintain and protect this property system, which is equivalent to saying that the state is the instrument of the property-owning class or classes to guarantee the social structure of which they are the beneficiaries.[2]

A certain theory of revolution follows logically from this theory of the state. The class(es) owning the means of production exploit the propertyless class(es) and are able to do so because of their control of the state as the instrument of coercion and repression. A revolution is therefore an act of the exploited class (or an alliance of exploited classes) to seize state power and institute a new property system expropriating the former owners and vesting ownership in the successful revolutionary class(es). The latter— or, if there are more than one, the dominant one in the alliance of revolutionary classes—now becomes the new ruling class.

Applied to the bourgeois revolution, this theory saw ranged against the feudal ruling class and its state an alliance between the rising bourgeoisie on the one hand and the oppressed peasantry and nascent proletariat on the other, with the bourgeoisie clearly the dominant partner. The revolution overthrew feudalism, dispossessing the nobility and substituting bourgeois private property in the means of production (especially land), with the new state as the guarantor of the now triumphant capitalist mode of production and exchange. The essence of the bourgeois revolution, in other words, was the replacement of one property system (feudal) by another (bourgeois).

It is probably safe to say that nearly all Marxists in the years before 1917 subscribed to this theory. To extend it to the next revolution, the proletarian revolution which would usher in the

new socialist society, was both logical and easy.* The main con-
tending classes, as the *Communist Manifesto* so eloquently argued,
were the bourgeoisie and the proletariat. The proletariat, as the
revolutionary class, would gain control of the state (peacefully
according to the reformists, violently according to the revolutionaries) and expropriate the bourgeoisie and big landowners.
Since, however, there could be no question of dividing up the
means of production among individual workers, the new property
system would necessarily have to be collective. And since the only
institution representing the working class as a whole would be the
new state, this meant that the erstwhile private property of the
bourgeoisie would become the property of the state. Thus, the
proletariat would become the new ruling class with its own state
through which it would become the owner of the means of production. On this basis the development of socialism could proceed.

The Russian Revolution appeared to conform to this theory.
The Bolsheviks, certainly a workers' party, seized control of the
state in the name of the proletariat, expropriated the bourgeoisie
(including the properties of foreign capitalists), grouped the
"commanding heights" of the economy (large-scale urban industry, transport, banking) into a more or less unified state-owned
sector, and proclaimed the establishment of a socialist society. To
be sure, the character of the revolution in the countryside, where
some four-fifths of the population lived, was rather different:
there the estates seized from the big landowners were parceled
out into millions of individual peasant holdings, remaining outside the control of the state and largely impervious to proletarian

---

*This is not to say that there were no serious differences among Marxists in that
period on the theory of the state. But they related not to the role of classes and the
centrality of the property system but rather to whether the revolutionary class
could take over and utilize for its purposes the existing state (thesis of the
reformists) or would have to smash the existing state and replace it with a new one
(thesis of the revolutionaries). There is no doubt, as Lenin conclusively proved in
The State and Revolution, that Marx himself held to the revolutionary thesis, which
explains why he and the Bolsheviks generally applied the label "revisionist" to
those adhering to the reformist thesis. But this dispute, despite its prominence
and bitterness, should not be allowed to obscure the far-reaching agreement
between the two factions on the basic meaning of revolution as the replacement of
one property system by another.

influences. But the peasants' share in political power was limited from the outset and did not last long. The question of their future role therefore seemed to be a problem of the new socialist society rather than an indication of its nonsocialist character.

The Trotskyist view of the Soviet Union was and is firmly rooted in this theory of the state and revolution. But there is one problem which arose quite early to challenge its validity. Marxist theory had all along maintained that any government in a class society, regardless of its specific form, is essentially a dictatorship of the ruling class over the ruled classes, and this would be no less true of a socialist society in which classes would necessarily persist for a long time, classlessness being a characteristic not of socialism but of the higher stage of communism. This is the origin of the theory of the dictatorship of the proletariat as the kind of transitional regime which would come to power with the revolution and preside over the transition from socialism to communism. But before the Russian Revolution, all Marxists not only agreed but insisted that this regime, while dictatorial vis-à-vis the old exploiting classes, would be the broadest kind of democracy for the workers, much more democratic than the most liberal of bourgeois democracies. Workers would have all the civil rights and liberties proclaimed by bourgeois revolutions but hitherto largely confined in practice to members of the bourgeoisie itself. Indeed it was only by exercising these rights and liberties that workers could transform themselves into new human beings capable of building a new society.

That such a functioning workers' democracy did not emerge in the period immediately following the October Revolution was certainly a disappointment to many; but at the same time it was easy enough to explain as due to the extremely difficult conditions of civil war and economic breakdown that characterized the years 1917–1921. Trotsky himself was one of the Bolshevik leaders who approved of and participated in the repressions of those years, by no means all of which were directed against reactionaries and counterrevolutionaries. But with the end of the civil war and the return to more normal economic conditions, the underlying theory would clearly have led one to expect a gradual spread and strengthening of democratic institutions and practices among the workers who, it must be remembered, were now supposed to constitute the ruling class.

But this did not happen. On the contrary, the very real seeds of workers' democracy which had been planted and begun to sprout prior to and during the revolution—the trade unions, the party organizations, the local soviets—now entered a period of decline which, with ups and downs, has continued to this day. These organizations, in the form in which they have survived, are rigidly controlled from the top, being mere executors of decisions made at the level of the Central Committee and the Politburo; the workers themselves—now more than 60 percent of the active population as against less than 15 percent in 1914—have no rights of self-organization, or self-expression, and of course that most basic of workers' rights, the right to strike, is totally suppressed.

This situation presents a fundamental challenge to the theory of state and revolution sketched above. If the proletariat is the new ruling class in the USSR, how does it happen that it has no say in who occupies the positions of power in the party and government; lacks organizations of its own; and is totally deprived even of any channels or methods of discussing and debating, let alone deciding, the great issues of politics, economics, and foreign policy which shape its life and will determine its future?

This is where the Trotskyist theory of the bureaucracy enters the picture. Its basic premise is that *objective* conditions prevailing in Russia after the revolution were such as to make impossible the direct assumption of power by the proletariat, not just for a few years but for a considerable period of time. The most important of these objective conditions, underlying all the others, was the underdeveloped state of the forces of production, implying a low level of education and culture, especially for the oppressed classes, and above all a universal state of scarcity. It was here, in this universal state of scarcity, that Trotsky located the breeding ground of "bureaucratism":

> While the first attempt [in the immediate aftermath of the seizure of power] to create a state cleansed of bureaucratism fell foul . . . of the unfamiliarity of the masses with self-government, the lack of qualified workers devoted to socialism, etc., it very soon after these immediate difficulties encountered others more profound. That

reduction of the state to functions of "accounting and control," with a continual narrowing of the function of compulsion, demanded by the party program, assumed at least a relative condition of general contentment. Just this necessary condition was lacking. No help came from the West. The power of the democratic Soviets proved cramping, even unendurable, when the task of the day was to accommodate those privileged groups whose existence was necessary for defense, for industry, for technique and science. In this decidedly not "socialistic" operation, taking from ten and giving to one, there crystallized out and developed a powerful caste of specialists in distribution.[3]

This "caste of specialists" was of course the bureaucracy. It grew and consolidated its power with the recovery and expansion of the Soviet economy, and its dominance in Soviet society was assured at least until the conditions which had given rise to it were fundamentally altered, i.e., until the proletariat had acquired the qualifications necessary to govern itself, and the condition of universal scarcity had been substantially alleviated. Even when that time would come—a subject we shall revert to presently—the bureaucracy would not voluntarily abdicate its power but would have to be removed by a second revolution. This second revolution, however, would not be a social revolution in the sense of the bourgeois revolutions of the seventeenth and eighteenth centuries or the 1917 revolution in Russia because it would not involve a change in the property system. Rather it would give to the property system installed by the October Revolution its real meaning. The proletariat which had made the revolution and replaced private by state ownership of the means of production would for the first time step forward as the active, self-conscious ruling class no longer in need of the services of the bureaucratic caretaker who had opportunistically taken on the job of managing the temporarily incapacitated proletariat's affairs and in the process arrogated to itself all manner of airs and privileges. The second revolution, in other words, would be the fulfillment and not the negation of the first.

An attractive theory, no doubt, with the special merit of allowing its adherents to hold onto the theory of the state and revolution with which they started without having recourse to the lies and deceptions of official Soviet ideology. But it suffers from certain defects which, benefiting from the wisdom of hindsight, I think we can now see are not only serious but fatal.

First, there is the obvious point that the longer the alleged rule of the bureaucracy lasts, the less convincing is the Trotskyist theory of its essential nature. The notion of a ruling class that never gets to rule but must always submit to the mistreatment and exactions of a caretaker regime of bureaucrats makes little sense. Either the second revolution comes and proves the correctness of the theory; or if it fails to come, the theory has to be abandoned and another put in its place. Postponing for a moment the question of the possible nature of this replacement theory, we should note, and indeed emphasize, that this conclusion is in full accord with the thinking of Trotsky himself, who never for a moment believed that the bureaucratic regime in the USSR was anything but a strictly temporary phenomenon. The following quotations from his 1939 article show how strongly he felt on this crucial point:

> Scientifically and politically . . . the question poses itself as follows: Does the bureaucracy represent a temporary growth on a social organism or has this growth already become transformed into an historically indispensable organ? Social excrescences can be the product of an "accidental" (i.e., temporary and extraordinary) enmeshing of historical circumstances. . . .
>
> If this war provokes, as we firmly believe, a proletarian revolution, it must inevitably lead to the overthrow of the bureaucracy in the USSR and regeneration of Soviet democracy on a far higher economic and cultural basis than in 1918. In that case the question as to whether the Stalinist bureaucracy was a "class" or a growth on the workers' state will be automatically solved. . . .
>
> If, however, it is conceded that the present war will provoke not revolution but a decline of the proletariat, then there remains another alternative: the further decay of monopoly capitalism, its further fusion with the state and the replacement of democracy wherever it still remained by a totalitarian regime. The inability of the proletariat to take into its hands the leadership of society could actually lead under these conditions to the growth of a new exploiting class from the Bonapartist fascist bureaucracy. This would be, according to all indications, a regime of decline, signalizing the eclipse of civilization.

The historic alternative, carried to the end, is as follows: either the Stalin regime is an abhorrent relapse in the process of transforming bourgeois society into a socialist society, or the Stalin regime is the first stage of a new exploiting society. If the second prognosis proves correct, then, of course, the bureaucracy will become a new exploiting class. . . .

The second imperialist war poses the unsolved task on a higher historical stage. It tests anew not only the stability of the existing regimes but also the ability of the proletariat to replace them. The results of this test will undoubtedly have a decisive significance for our appraisal of the modern epoch as the epoch of proletarian revolution. If contrary to all probabilities the October Revolution fails during the course of the present war, or immediately thereafter, to find its continuation in any of the advanced countries; and if, on the contrary, the proletariat is thrown back everywhere and on all fronts—then we should doubtlessly have to revise our conception of the present epoch and its driving forces. In that case it would be a question not of slapping a copybook label on the USSR or the Stalinist gang but of re-evaluating the world historical perspective for the next decades if not centuries: Have we entered the epoch of social revolution and socialist society, or on the contrary the epoch of the declining society of totalitarian bureaucracy?[4]

It would be wrong to treat these passages as one would a carefully thought-out theoretical assessment or analysis. Trotsky was obviously excited by the beginning of the war. The hour of truth was approaching for the USSR, and perhaps for him personally as well. He had no doubt about the outcome: just as World War I had given rise to the Russian Revolution, so World War II would generate its continuation, this time in the heartlands of capitalism to which Trotsky had always looked for the support and guidance which would enable Russia to overcome its crippling backwardness. The miserable Stalinist bureaucracy would surely be burned out in the crucible of revolution, and on its ashes would rise a liberated workers' state fulfilling the democratic promise of 1917.

This was the basic message Trotsky sought to convey to his followers. The very language bespeaks his optimism and confidence. Elsewhere in the article he even goes so far as to ask (my emphasis): "Might we not place ourselves in a ludicrous position if we affixed to the Bonapartist oligarchy the nomenclature of a new ruling class *just a few years or even a few months prior to its inglorious downfall?*" Victory may be nearer, much nearer, than you think!

In this context the dire forebodings as to what to expect in the case of the failure of the revolution should be interpreted not as probabilities, let alone predictions, but as aspects of an exhortation to the faithful to step up their preparedness and redouble their commitment to the cause. Trotsky was never one to make a sharp distinction between scientific analysis and inspirational propaganda, and this is a pretty clear case of the primacy of the latter over the former. Still, the way he formulated the alternatives undoubtedly does reveal a great deal about his basic theoretical position. The overwhelming likelihood, amounting to a new certainty, was for a successful proletarian revolution. But if "contrary to all probabilities" this should fail, then the prognosis was clear and unambiguous: as far as the USSR was concerned, the Stalin regime would have to be interpreted as the first stage of a new exploiting society and "then, of course, the bureaucracy will become a new exploiting class." At the same time, the world as a whole would be entering the "declining society of totalitarian bureaucracy." A third conceivable alternative, the continuation of the existing state of affairs, was not mentioned and probably never even entered Trotsky's head. The USSR had come to a crossroads: either the revolution of 1917 would be fulfilled, or it would be defeated and on its ruins would grow up a new exploitative society.

Against this background the restatement of the Trotskyist position by Ernest Mandel, sixty years after the October Revolution and more than thirty years after World War II, comes as a distinct anticlimax. Mandel repeats all the familiar themes, stressing the centrality of the system of state ownership of the means of production and claiming to have demonstrated that "our definition of the Soviet Union as a bureaucratically degenerate workers' state [is] correct both historically and theoretically."[5] He does not allude to Trotsky's view in 1939 that if the October Revolution should fail to find its continuation during or immediately after the war, "of course" the bureaucracy would become a new exploiting

class. His way around this awkward problem is simply to pose
anew the question of the durability of the bureaucratic regime:

> What remains open is the question of whether the victory of the
> proletarian revolution in the industrially advanced countries, or in
> which the proletariat already represents the absolute majority of
> the nation, will unleash—both within these countries and on a
> world scale—a process than can "de-bureaucratize" the experience
> of the proletarian revolutions of the twentieth century with a
> rapidity much more disconcerting than the duration of the phe-
> nomenon of bureaucratization itself. Here, history will have the last
> word. Should it confirm that revolutionary Marxists have been
> harboring illusions on this subject, then it would be necessary to
> draw conclusions about the deeper historical roots of bureaucrati-
> zation different from those generally drawn in the analysis of
> Marx, Lenin, Trotsky, and the Fourth International. But it is
> unjustified, impressionistic, and irresponsible to draw these conclu-
> sions prematurely, before the evidence is in.[6]

Apparently Trotsky was *very* premature when he stated that
these conclusions would have to be drawn from the consequences
of World War II. But Mandel offers no reason to suppose that a
more decisive test is in the offing, now or in the visible future. The
evidence just is not yet in, he says; and so far as the theory is
concerned, it looks as though it never will be unless or until the
long-delayed second revolution actually comes.

Let us concede, for the sake of argument, that history has not
yet had its last word; still, shouldn't more attention be paid to
what history has been saying? For example, what about the Soviet
regime's more than three decades of survival since World War II?
There were crises, to be sure, especially in the Soviet "empire,"
but they have been no more severe than crises suffered by the
older capitalist empires, and it would be absurd to maintain that
the existence of the regime has at any time been in danger. On the
contrary, both economically and militarily the Soviet Union has
steadily grown in strength, and the regime's capacity to control
this increasing power and use it in its own interest has never been
less open to question.

A particularly important test for the "bureaucracy" theory, I
think, was Stalin's death and its consequences. According to the

theory, Stalin was the ideal bureaucrat and his rule as absolute dictator, combining the stick of terror with the carrot of special material privileges, was crucial to the character and indeed the very survival of the regime. Given this premise, it was to be expected that Stalin's death would not only precipitate a crisis of the regime but makes continuation in anything like its then existing form impossible. It is against this background that we must interpret the remarkable, and in their way brilliant, series of writings devoted to post-Stalin Russia in the mid-1950s by Isaac Deutscher, undoubtedly the most eminent Trotskyist historian of that period.[7]

Deutscher starts from a view of the USSR in the period 1917–1953 which is identical in all essentials to that put forward by Trotsky in *The Revolution Betrayed*. The working class was strong enough to seize power in 1917 but too weak by the end of the civil war to play the part of a ruling class. This enabled the bureaucracy to step into the breach and to rule under Stalin's increasingly absolute dictatorship. But the logic of the bureaucracy's rule stemmed from the property system established by the revolution. The result was a very rapid development of the forces of production (size and educational level of the labor force, science and technology, etc.) and a considerable though smaller rise in the general standard of living. However, as the complexity of the economy increased and the cultural level of the masses rose, the rule of the bureaucracy, with its brutal ways and lack of flexibility and initiative, became increasingly counterproductive. By the time of Stalin's death in 1953, with recovery from the ravages of World War II largely accomplished, the situation had already reached crisis proportions. Deutscher was of the opinion that Stalin's henchmen, though afraid to move against him while he was still alive, were very much aware of the true state of affairs and recognized that their own survival depended on the carrying through of far-reaching reforms.

Deutscher was fascinated by the problem—for which he cited historical precedents, including that of the reform of the papacy in the early sixteenth century—of how dyed-in-the-wool Stalinists could reform the very system they had helped to create and in whose misdeeds they were heavily implicated. All of his writings in this period dwell on this problem, emphasizing the complexities and ambiguities of the process under way but finally concluding that through it all the reform movement was following a histori-cal logic of its own which could end only by radically transforming Soviet society for the better. A few quotations from "The Meaning of De-Stalinization" (1956) in *Ironies of History* will convey the tenor of his thought:

> If the "liberal trend" is defined as a radical lessening of govern-mental coercion and a striving for government by consent, then this trend has been obviously and even conspicuously at work in Soviet society. . . .
>
> With public ownership of the means of production firmly estab-lished, with the consolidation and expansion of planned economy, and—last but not least—with the traditions of a socialist revolution alive in the minds of its people, the Soviet Union breaks with Stalinism in order to resume its advance towards equality and socialist democracy. . . .
>
> In a society whose political consciousness has been atomized or reduced to amorphousness, any major political change, if there is an overwhelming social need for it, can come only from the ruling group. This is precisely what has happened in Russia. No matter how much one may dislike Stalin's epigones, one must acknowledge that they have proved themselves capable of a much more sensi-tive response to the need for reform than was generally expected of them. . . .
>
> The present degree of liberalization is probably just sufficient to allow some scope for new processes of political thought and opinion-formation to develop in the intelligentsia and the working class. By their nature these are molecular processes, which require time to mature. But once they have matured they are certain to transform profoundly the whole moral and political climate of communism, and to transform it in a spirit of socialist democracy.[8]

In terms of Trotsky's theory of the bureaucracy, what Deutscher was saying was that the bureaucracy had reached the predicted stage at which, having fulfilled its task as stand-in for the working class, it not only could be dispensed with but would have to go if further progress was to be made. But he appeared to be adding something new, that the leadership of the bureaucracy under-stood the untenability of its position and, while desperately striving to save itself, was in fact in the process of committing suicide. Once again in terms of the theory, he seemed to be saying that the second revolution which Trotsky had also predicted was actually happening, though, contrary to what Trosky had expected, in a peaceful and reformist way. But Deutscher backed off from actually drawing this conclusion:

> Whether the change and replacement of ruling groups and gen-erations will proceed gradually and peacefully or through violent convulsions and irreconcilable conflict is a question which need hardly and can hardly be resolved *a priori.* The whole development is quite unprecedented; and there are too many unknowns in the equations. One can at the most analyze the conditions under which the change, or the series of changes, can run its course in a rela-tively peaceful and reformist manner; and those under which the reformist phase would prove to be a mere prelude to violent up-heaval. The subject is too large, complex, and speculative to be tackled in this contribution.[9]

So far as I know, Deutscher did not return to this problem in his later writings, and interest in the likelihood of peaceful reform in the Soviet Union soon faded. The last word on this chapter in the interpretation of Soviet history may be left to Daniel Singer, a younger friend of Deutscher's and a worthy continuator of his work. Discussing at a colloquium in 1977 the theme of "Weak-nesses and Potentialities of Dissidence in the USSR," Singer recalled to his listeners the "already somewhat ancient controversy on the nature of changes in post-Stalinist Russia":

> Will they come from above or from below, from the summit or from the base, from inside or outside the party. . . . In their more sophisticated versions, the gradualist or Fabian theses counted not only on the good will of the reformers, they also combined with this factor the social constraints and the pressure from the base as forces setting in motion in Russia a return journey along the road which had led from the dictatorship of the proletariat to that of the Secretary General. This controversy has now been left behind. Even before the fall of Khrushchev, and certainly since the invasion of Czechoslovakia, it has become evident that the system has its own logic, the apparatus its instinct for survival, and that it will not hesitate to strike out without pity if its interests are at stake.[10]

It was understandable that a proponent of the Trotsky theory of the bureaucracy should err as Deutscher did in the mid-50s. What is not so understandable is that the theory should be repeated in 1978 by a leading Trotskyist theorist like Mandel, not only without significant change but without paying any attention to the crucially important events surrounding and following the departure of Stalin from the scene.

One more point on what history has been saying about the character of Soviet society. According to the Trotskyist theory as interpreted by Mandel, the proletariat is still the ruling class. This follows in syllogistic fashion from the nature of the property system. Historically, ruling classes have been property-owning classes. But given the fact of state ownership of the means of production, there are no property-owning classes in the USSR. The means of production are owned by the whole society through the state, and the overwhelming majority of the society are workers. Therefore the workers are the ruling class. Q.E.D. But Mandel knows as well as anyone that this legalistic interpretation is totally at odds with the realities of Soviet life. At one point he goes so far as to say: "Obviously, from simple common sense it is absurd to say that the dictatorship of the proletariat exists in the Soviet Union, since the immense majority of the proletariat exercises not only no dictatorship but not even any power."[11] But the problem goes a lot deeper. At one time, back in Trotsky's day, it was possible to argue that the Russian proletariat, with the experience of the revolution still in the recent past, felt that it had won the right to be the ruling class, that it was being deprived of the fruits of its victory, and that it would assert its supremacy as soon as circumstances permitted. There was even a strong trace of this line of thought in Deutscher's writings. But not in Mandel's. Here we find a realistic—and I think accurate—recognition of profound changes in the existential situation of the Soviet workers:

> The Soviet working class has been profoundly disappointed by the way the October Revolution turned, through the Stalinist degeneration, towards a model of socialist leadership which does not meet the workers' needs. The workers have not been attracted to the capitalist model either. But they see no alternative in the world today, no third model. . . . In the absence of any such alternative

model, there has been a withdrawal towards private life, immediate demands, higher living standards, even towards individual social advancement. . . . All these forms of withdrawal are practically inevitable. The second major reason [for the quiescence of the Russian workers] is that there has been undeniable progress in the standard of living and working conditions of the Soviet workers. This progress, nearly constant since the death of Stalin, i.e., over the past twenty-five years, has generated what may be called a climate within the working class that is more reformist than revolutionary. . . . Normally . . . the Soviet workers hope to improve their lot by exerting pressure within the framework of the system rather than by challenging it comprehensively.[12]

It seems to me that this diagnosis of the situation of the Soviet proletariat puts the final nail in the coffin of the Trotskyist theory of the bureaucracy as the temporary stand-in for a ruling working class. A reformist working class is one which accepts the system, however grudgingly and unenthusiastically. And the very essence of the system is the subordination of the working class, the producers of the social product and its surplus, to an external power which has grown to monstrous dimensions since it came into existence more than sixty years ago. To go on denying that this power represents and is controlled by a new ruling class flies in the face of reality and invites hopeless theoretical confusion.

Here we meet what would presumably be Mandel's last line of defense:

If one were to assert that the relations of production in the Soviet Union are neither socialist nor capitalist but those of a new society dominated by an exploiting class, one would have to demonstrate the origins of this mysterious ruling class, which is completely nonexistent up to zero hour, when it seizes power. One would have to uncover the dynamic, the laws of development of this society— something which none of the proponents of this theory have ever been capable of doing. It would also have to be shown that these relations of production, allegedly characteristic of a new mode of production, have the stability and capacity for self-reproduction common to modes of production, which is contrary to everything we know about Soviet society.[13]

The problem here, however, is real only for one who is trapped by a rigidified version of the Marxist theory of the state. A pre-revolutionary society is characterized by a certain class structure which includes a ruling class and a revolutionary class. The latter overthrows the former. The revolutionary class goes on to become the new ruling class. The old ruling class either succeeds in making a counterrevolution or dies out. The only variation allowed for in this scenario is that if the revolutionary class is for some reason not ready or able to perform its new role, a bureaucracy may take over in its place until it *is* ready, whereupon the interrupted drama proceeds according to the original script. No other developments are possible, no new classes are allowed to emerge.

The answer to this was given, however unwittingly, by Trotsky himself long ago (in the passage from the 1939 article cited above): "If the Stalin regime," he said, "is the first stage of a new exploiting society . . . then, of course, the bureaucracy will become a new exploiting class." In other words, *the new exploiting class develops out of the conditions created by the revolution itself.* This is of course not a problem which interested Trotsky, since he was firmly convinced that it would never arise in reality. But it is not at all excluded from his theoretical vision, and it is hard to see why Mandel should find it so mystifying.

As for the laws of development of this society, Mandel undoubtedly has a point that they have not been satisfactorily worked out. On the other hand, recent reinterpretations of Soviet history—most notably Charles Bettelheim's *Class Struggles in the USSR*, two volumes of which have appeared to date—have started to lay the foundations for serious, if long overdue, study of the workings of Soviet society. And certainly Bettelheim and others have already provided us with rich materials for tracing and analyzing the birth, growth, and maturation of the new ruling class to which it has given rise. Finally, with regard to the "stability and capacity for self-reproduction common to modes of production," what more evidence does Mandel require beyond the society's survival and ascent to the status of superpower in the not exactly tranquil period from 1917 to 1978?

(October 1978)

* * * *

The foregoing critique of the Trotskyist theory of the nature of
the Soviet society, as first put forward by Trotsky himself and
more recently defended by Ernest Mandel, was subsequently
answered by Mandel; and this answer was in turn the subject of
a rejoinder by me (*Monthly Review,* July-August 1979). On the
whole, Mandel reaffirmed his position without adding anything
essentially new. But in so doing he convinced me that my critique
was incomplete and insufficiently explicit on certain important
points. I think it is therefore useful to add the following, con-
densed from the rejoinder to Mandel.

(1) Mandel's reply is entitled "Why the Soviet Bureaucracy Is
Not a Ruling Class," clearly implying that my position is that
the bureaucracy *is* a ruling class. This is not so. In my opinion
the bureaucracy is neither a class nor does it rule. To be sure,
if the term is interpreted, as it often is, to mean all those who staff
the agencies and apparatuses of the state, then of course it is a
mere tautology to say that the bureaucracy rules. But Mandel
does not fall into this trap. Instead he defines the bureaucracy "to
include . . . all the layers in Soviet society that are privileged in
one way or another," going on to note that this means that

> we are talking about millions of people: between five and ten
> million, if not more. This total would include the entire trade union
> bureaucracy; the whole officer corps of the armed forces, not just
> the generals and marshals; the entire hierarchy of production, not
> just the directors but also the engineers; and the great majority of
> the intelligentsia (except teachers, who are paid less than workers
> and have no material privileges).[14]

Now, I have no doubt that those who control the Soviet state are
to be found among the privileged layers of the society, but I fail to
see what sense it makes to lump together all these heterogeneous
groups—undoubtedly riddled with conflicts of interest over shar-
ing the privileges—into a collectivity called the "bureaucracy"
which is supposed to play the role assigned to it by Mandel's theory.

If one were to reply that these groups act through the party to
control the state, one would have to show that there is some
systematic connection between them and the party such as would

exist, for example, if party members were elected on the basis of a franchise in effect limited to the privileged layers. But of course no such connection exists: the party is a self-reproducing organization which at no time has been subjected, either in theory or in practice, to any form of outside control. If the party can nevertheless be said to "represent" the privileged layers, it does so out of its own choice and in its own way; it certainly cannot be said to be their instrument. Under the circumstances I cannot see that Mandel's broadening of the concept of bureaucracy provides us with a meaningful concept of bureaucratic rule.

If the proletariat is manifestly not the ruling class and rule by "bureaucracy" is either a trivial or a meaningless concept, then the only alternative is that there is a new ruling class in the Soviet Union. Without attempting to explore this question in detail here, I will only note that it has two aspects, one theoretical and one empirical. We need a carefully articulated theory of class which goes beyond the familiar Marxian view (as formulated by Lenin) that "classes are large groups of people distinguished by the place they occupy in a historically defined system of social production, by their role vis-à-vis the means of production, by their role in the social organization of labor, and by the modes of obtaining and the importance of the share of social wealth of which they dispose." The theory needs also to encompass at least the following: the formation of classes in conflict with other classes, the character and degree of their self-consciousness, their internal organizational structures, the ways in which they generate and utilize ideologies to further their interests, and their modes of reproduction and self-perpetuation. And the empirical task of course is to use the theory as the basis for collecting and analyzing the available material on class formation and class struggles in the USSR since the October Revolution.

Mandel believes, as I do, that the ability to reproduce itself and perpetuate its existence is essential to the idea of a ruling class, and he argues that precisely this ability is what the group in power in the Soviet Union lacks. If this could really be demonstrated, I would have to agree that there is no ruling class in the USSR: this is therefore a crucial test. But the only evidence he offers is that "there is no guarantee for a bureaucrat that he or she will remain a bureaucrat. There is even less guarantee that his or her sons and daughters will remain bureaucrats." True enough, but I must remind the reader that I do not identify bureaucrat (either in the narrow sense or in the broad sense of a privileged person) with a member of the ruling class. I would include in the ruling class only the upper echelons of the party, state, and military apparatuses.[15] And I would argue that they are drawn from a reasonably homogeneous group with all the essential attributes of a class, including the ability to reproduce itself (through the way they socialize their offspring, through differential access to education, through networks of "connections," even through the formal device of the *nomenklatura**). It is of course true that the factual basis for these statements is not as well documented as one could wish. Officially controlled societies like the Soviet Union, while not averse to Western-style sociological studies of their middle strata, are extremely secretive when it comes to the top and bottom extremes.† Nevertheless, a fairly clear general picture can be pieced together from various types of evidence (the Soviet press and literature, accounts of dissidents, observations of foreign reporters and visitors), and it unmistakably points to the existence of a deeply class-divided society in which consciousness of the "we-they" division on both sides of the great divide is at

---

*The *nomenklatura* has a double meaning: on the one hand it is a list of high-level posts which can be filled only on the nomination of the party center, and on the other hand it is a list of persons maintained by the party center (mostly but not entirely party members) who can be nominated to fill these posts. Through this device, that segment of the ruling group which is, so to speak, on active duty is wholly self-reproducing and carefully insulated from unwanted pressure from lower-level bureaucrats in the usual meaning of the term, as well as from rank-and-file members of the party.

†Murray Yanowitch, author of an excellent monograph based on Soviet sociological studies, remarks: "It hardly needs to be said that we will seek in vain for Soviet studies of movement into or out of a 'ruling class,' a 'bureaucratic elite,' a group of 'controllers,' or an 'underclass.' " See *Social and Economic Inequality in the Soviet Union: Six Studies* (White Plains, N.Y.: M. E. Sharpe, 1977), p. 104. Occasionally, however, the Soviet satirical journal *Krokodil* casts a sharp beam of light on forbidden subjects: for example, the *New York Times* of March 6, 1978, reproduces a cartoon from *Krokodil* showing an arrogant-looking cigarette-smoking brat being lectured in the "children's room of a militia station." The caption, according to the *Times,* reads: "Hey, take it easy! Don't forget whose son you are talking to!"

least as strong as it is in Western capitalist societies. (Is it necessary
to add that the division of society into classes does not preclude,
either theoretically or historically, mobility across class lines in
both upward and downward directions? In fact, as Marx was at
pains to emphasize, the strongest and most dangerous ruling
classes are precisely those which best know how to co-opt and
integrate into their own ranks the ablest and most vigorous
members of the dominated classes.)

(2) Beyond the question of the present structure of Soviet
society, there is the problem of the direction in which it is likely to
move in the future. Mandel, like Trotsky before him, does not
believe in the possibility of socialist development except in the
advanced capitalist countries, and he expects them (after they
have become socialist) to provide the necessary economic and
political support to enable not only the Soviet Union but also the
entire Third World to embark on the socialist road. This can be
either an optimistic or a pessimistic perspective depending on
how one rates the chances of a revolution in the West in the
foreseeable future. Mandel, being an optimist, rates these chances
very high indeed, going so far as to interpret working-class
struggles in the West "over the last century or so" as the "proletariat's periodic spontaneous attempts to reconstruct society
along socialist lines." This reading of the history of the last century seems to me to be a tribute to the human mind's ability to
believe what it wants to in the face of overwhelming evidence to
the contrary, but to pursue this theme would obviously take us far
beyond the scope of this discussion. Nor would it serve my present purpose, which is simply to point out that Trotskyism in its
Mandelian version is solidly in the tradition of Western-centered
thought which has spawned a rich and variegated offspring,
including the renaissance, the reformation, the enlightenment,
and more recently racism and imperialism. What these have in
common is a belief in the unique creativity of Europe and hence
the superiority of its civilization. It can be said quite correctly that
Marxism is also an offspring of Western-centered thought. But
there is the difference that Marxism, especially as Marx himself
was shaping it in his later years, had the potential to transcend its
European origins and to become a truly universal world outlook.[16]

True, Marxism remained very much a Western-centered movement in the period between Marx's death and the Russian Revolution, a fact which reflected the economic and even more the political realities of the time. But after the October Revolution, as Lenin alone among the great Marxist thinkers of that generation sensed, Marxism increasingly overflowed its European boundaries and reached out to fulfill its universal mission.[17] And after World War II with the victory of the Chinese Revolution and the flowering of Marxism not only in Asia but also in Latin America and Africa, Marxism came to full maturity as the revolutionary outlook of the most exploited workers and peasants on a world scale. Simultaneously, and connected with this process in a cause-and-effect relationship, there took place the maturing of capitalism not as a collection of discrete societies in various stages of development but as a thoroughly integrated global system dominated by the double dialectic of center/periphery and development/underdevelopment.

Not all the implications of these momentous developments are visible yet—far from it. And our ability to analyze and understand them is still at a primitive stage. But I think that one thing at any rate is clear: Western-centered Marxism, like Western-centered thought in general, is rapidly becoming more of a hindrance than help in getting on with this vitally important task.

(February 1980)

9
A CRISIS
IN MARXIAN THEORY

I am sure that many of you are familiar with Thomas Kuhn's little book *The Structure of Scientific Revolutions,* which has had an important and salutary effect on ways of looking at and analyzing the history of the natural sciences, and which has also aroused considerable interest among social scientists.[1]

Kuhn challenges the traditional view that science develops through a gradual process of accretion, with a host of theorists and researchers building up the scientific edifice a few bricks at a time and always on the basis of the accomplishments of their predecessors. Not so, says Kuhn: science develops through a series of revolutions, each rejecting much that has gone before and starting on new foundations. His key concept is that of the "paradigm," which means roughly a way of looking at reality—or that part of reality which falls within the scope of a given science. To take the best known example, the paradigm of the cosmos which dominated human thought for thousands of years was geocentric, with all the heavenly bodies being assumed to move around a fixed earth as its center. Astronomy based on this paradigm was developed and codified in the Ptolemaic system and held the field until the Copernican revolution, which abandoned the geocentric for a heliocentric paradigm.

Kuhn's idea is that when a new paradigm takes over—never, incidentally, without a struggle—it provides room for a more or less lengthy period of what he calls "normal science," i.e., the work of scientists who accept the new paradigm and seek to answer the questions and solve the problems which it poses or allows to be raised. But after a while "anomalies" begin to crop up—observations or research results which do not square with the paradigm and cannot be explained in terms of the normal science to which it gives rise. What then happens is that efforts are made to elaborate and complicate the paradigm so that it will accommodate the anomalies, a process resulting in an increasingly messy collection of ad hoc additions and exceptions (as in the proliferation and modification of epicycles by post-Ptolemy astronomers), culminating in a scientific crisis. The way out is then found—usually by persons not trained in the accepted ways of perceiving and doing things—in a revolution which establishes a new paradigm. The whole process of normal science–anomalies–crisis–revolution then repeats itself. (I might add that this way of viewing and analyzing the history of science is very congenial to Marxism, though Kuhn himself is far from being a radical: there have long been conservative as well as radical dialectical thinkers.)

I want to suggest that Marxism, considered as a science of history and society, has in certain important respects reached a stage of crisis in Kuhn's sense. The underlying paradigm, together with the normal science to which it gave rise, have in the course of the last century produced an interpretation of the history of the modern world which is enormously powerful and which has had a profound influence far beyond the community of Marxists.

In barest outline, this interpretation sees the history of the modern world from roughly the beginning of the sixteenth century as consisting of the following major, and to some degree overlapping, stages: (1) the emergence of capitalism as the dominant mode of production (primitive accumulation plus bourgeois revolutions in the core countries); (2) the mercantilist stage of capitalism; (3) the competitive industrial stage of capitalism under British hegemony; (4) the monopoly imperialist stage of capitalism beginning in the last quarter of the nineteenth century; (5) the global crisis of capitalism-imperialism beginning with World War I; (6) the spreading proletarian revolution beginning with the Russian Revolution of 1917, and the emergence and spread of socialism as successor to capitalism and transition to the communist society of the future.

The foundations of this interpretation of the history of the modern world were laid in the pre-1848 writings of Marx and Engels (especially *The German Ideology* and the *Communist Manifesto*). Theoretical deepening and elaboration came in the first volume of *Capital* (published in 1867). And the edifice was extended, amplified, and in a sense completed by the great revolutionary leaders of the twentieth century, Lenin and Mao Tsetung.

It is a magnificent intellectual and scientific creation—far superior to anything achieved by bourgeois social science, if indeed we may use that term at all, considering that at least since the beginnings of the global crisis of capitalism bourgeois thinkers have been vastly more concerned with ideological justification of the system than with scientific understanding of it history and future. But—and this is the point I want to emphasize—as history unfolds in the closing decades of the twentieth century, we are finding more and more anomalies in the Kuhnian sense, i.e., deviations between observed reality and the expectations generated by the theory.

Obviously I couldn't attempt to explore all these anomalies in the space available to me, and to tell the truth the task would in any case be far beyond my ability. But I do want to draw attention to what I think is probably the most important of these anomalies. For Marx, socialism was a transitional society between capitalism and communism. While he purposely refrained from drawing up blueprints, there is no doubt about what he considered the most fundamental characteristics of communism: it would be a classless society, a stateless society, and a society of genuine and not merely formal or legal equality among nationalities, races, sexes, and individuals. These goals would certainly be very long term in nature and might never be fully achieved. But just as certainly they establish guidelines and rough measuring rods. Only a society genuinely dedicated to these goals and shaping its practice accordingly can be considered socialist in the Marxian meaning of the term.

Now, as I have already indicated, the generally accepted Marxian interpretation of modern history leads us to expect that capitalism will be overthrown by proletarian revolutions, and that these revolutions will establish socialist societies. The theory, in fact, is so taken for granted as a reliable clue to what is happening in the world that every society which originates in a proletarian (or proletarian-led) revolution is automatically assumed to be and identified as a socialist society.

And this is where the anomalies begin. None of these "socialist" societies behave as Marx—and I think most Marxists up until quite recently—thought they would. They have not eliminated classes except in a purely verbal sense; and, except in the period of the Cultural Revolution in China, they have not attempted to follow a course which could have the long-run effect of eliminating classes. The state has not disappeared—no one could expect it to, except in a still distant future—but on the contrary has become more and more the central and dominant institution of society. Each interprets proletarian internationalism to mean support of its own interests and policies as interpreted by itself. They go to war not only in self-defense but to impose their will on other countries—even ones that are also assumed to be socialist.

All of this, I think, is now fairly obvious, and of course it is raising havoc among socialists and communists. I think it is no exaggeration to say that by now the anomalies have become so massive and egregious that the result has been a deep crisis in Marxian theory.

What is the way out? One way, which is clearly being taken by some Marxists, is to throw out the whole theory, abandon Marxism altogether, and retire into a state of agnosticism and cynicism—if not worse. But the trouble with this is that Marxism works as well as ever—and I would even say better—as a way of understanding the development of global capitalism and its crises: the particular anomalies I have been alluding to have no bearing on the validity of Marxism in this crucially important sphere. The part of Marxism that needs to be put on a new basis is that which deals with the post-revolutionary societies (with which, of course, Marx and Engels had no experience).

We do not need to rule out the *possiblity* of a post-revolutionary society's being socialist in the Marxian sense. That would be foolish and self-defeating. But we do need to recognize that a proletarian revolution can give rise to a nonsocialist society. I believe that it is only in this way that we can lay the basis for eliminating the disturbing anomalies I have been discussing.

Having recognized this, we can then proceed along one of two lines: (1) the hypothesis that the only alternative to socialism is capitalism, and (2) the hypothesis that proletarian revolutions can give rise to a new form of society, neither capitalist nor socialist. I believe that the second line is the fruitful one. The trouble with the capitalist hypothesis is that it quickly leads to as many anomalies as the socialist hypothesis. I said a minute ago that none of the so-called socialist societies behaves as Marx thought they would. Much the same can be said, only more so, if they are assumed to be capitalist societies: Marxists know a lot about the way capitalism works, and none of the post-revolutionary societies conforms to the pattern. They have plenty of contradictions of their own, but they do not take the same form as the contradictions of capitalism. If this is so—and I don't know of anyone who claims to be able to analyze their development in terms of capitalism's "laws of motion"—how can calling them capitalist lead to anything but confusion and frustration?

The new-society hypothesis, on the other hand, while not telling us anything about how these societies function, does pose exciting challenges for scientific work—and inevitably has profound implications for political practice. I firmly believe that it points to the path we should follow and offers us the best hope of resolving the crisis of Marxian theory which is now visibly tearing the international revolutionary movement apart.

(June 1979)

10
POST-REVOLUTIONARY SOCIETY

Much of this book has been concerned with what post-revolutionary society, exemplified mainly by the Soviet Union, is not, rather than what it is. I have argued that it is neither capitalism nor socialism as these social formations have been traditionally understood by Marxists, nor is it, as Trotskyists maintain, a transitional society between the two which has been temporarily stalled by a bureaucratic deformation. It is, in my opinion, a society with enough basic differences from both capitalism and socialism to be considered and studied as a new social formation in its own right. In this chapter I venture what I have not previously attempted in print, to sketch with very broad strokes what appear to me to be the fundamental characteristics of this new social formation, to identify what distinguishes it from these other social formations. In doing so, however, I must stress, first, that I consider what follows to be provisional as a whole and in detail; and second, that while I believe the Soviet Union to be a valid prototype of other presently existing revolutionary societies, I do not mean to preclude the possibility that some of them, and others still to come, are following or will follow a different road.

The starting point is capitalism, which gave rise to all the social sciences with which we are familiar today. The economic foundation of capitalism has three determining characteristics: (1) ownership of the means of production by private capitalists; (2) separation of the total social capital into many competing or potentially competing units; and (3) production of the great bulk of commodities (both goods and services) by workers who, owning no means of production of their own, are obliged to sell their labor power to capitalists in order to acquire the means of subsistence. In Soviet-type societies, two of these three determining characteristics have been eliminated. Most of the means of production are owned by the state or, in the case of the collective farms which are formally cooperatives, closely controlled by the state. And the units into which they are divided for managerial and administrative purposes are not autonomous and do not relate to each other in the manner of competing capitals. Instead they form parts of a hierarchical structure of decision-making and control which reaches its peak in the top political organs of the state. The guiding force in this system is therefore an overall plan which, however well or badly articulated, is a set of directives having the force of law and not merely, as under capitalism, indicators designed to help the autonomous units of capital to act more rationally in their own interest.

The third determining characteristic of capitalism—production by propertyless wage laborers—is retained in the Soviet-type system, but with a significant difference. The Russian Revolution which brought this system into being, and later anticapitalist revolutions as well, was made in the name of the workers and peasants and its battles were fought by these same oppressed and exploited classes. In the early years of the new system their status both economically and politically was significantly improved. Among their most important gains was full employment and constitutional guarantees of the right to a job. In other words, Soviet workers, unlike workers under capitalism, cannot be fired by managements except in extreme circumstances: they have what in the United States is called tenure and is reserved for relatively small and generally privileged segments of the salaried work force.*

---

*In Japan the equivalent arrangement is "life employment" which is enjoyed by many more people than have tenure in the United States but who still constitute a minority of the employed population. Most of the other advanced capitalist countries probably fall between the United States and Japan in this respect. These partial guarantees of employment, which are not necessarily legally enforcable, scarcely affect the ability of the separate units of capital, and still less of the capitalist class as a whole, to vary the amount of employment offered in response to the requirements of the economic conjuncture. And it is precisely in this respect that the situation in the Soviet-type economies is basically different.

This job security, won through revolutionary struggles and sacrifices, is so precious to workers that no post-revolutionary regime would dare to abolish it regardless of what advantages, from the point of view of overall economic flexibility, might be gained by doing so. One can even say that the claims of post-revolutionary regimes to legitimacy depend to a very large extent on the job-security system.

The functioning of capitalism is governed by economic "laws" which are generated by the mutual interaction of competing capitals on the one hand, and of capitalists and wage laborers on the other. No overall direction exists or is needed: the system runs itself as long as capitalists act to maximize their profits and use their profits to expand their capitals. The state is of course involved in the process as the guarantor of the underlying property system and enforcer of the rules of the competitive struggle, and it also typically plays a role in strengthening the hand of some interests against others, and in attempting to resolve or ameliorate the contradictions to which the system periodically and/or irregularly gives rise. But in the economic sphere the state is dragged along by the laws of value and capital accumulation and the special interests they create. To use a mathematical analogy, the economy is the independent variable, the state the dependent variable.

It is the other way around in the Soviet-type system. True, the laws of value and capital accumulation keep operating to the extent that private enterprise and free markets are allowed to continue in existence, but this is mostly in the production and sale of agricultural products from the peasants' private plots which, while important for the supply of certain foods, is a minor aspect of the economy as a whole. It is also doubtless true that the individual production units in the state sector, as well as the ministries to which they are responsible, may and often do strive to act as profit-maximizers and capital-accumulators, but the extent to which they can actually play these roles is strictly limited by the planning system and subject to control by higher political authorities who hire and fire ministers and in the final analysis establish the norms which govern their conduct. The point to be emphasized is *not* that all manifestations of capitalist behavior patterns have been eliminated from Soviet-type societies—far from it—but that these have ceased to *dominate* the functioning of the economy and hence, indirectly, to shape the objectives and tasks of political power. In capitalist society the state is the servant of the economy; in Soviet-type societies it is the master.

I shall return to this subject below. Here I want only to add that this reversal of the economic/political relationship characteristic of capitalism in no way means or implies that in Soviet-type societies the state can do what it pleases, that it is released from economic constraints, that its behavior is not in the final analysis determined by economic considerations. I make no such claims; nor do I call into question the broad generalizations of historical materialism. I want only to argue that the historically unique set of socioeconomic relations which determine the specific form of the economic/political nexus under capitalism no longer exists in Soviet-type societies and has been replaced by a different one which, since it lacks an autonomous economic base, is formally akin to that which existed in feudal and other precapitalist societies.

In Soviet-type societies most consumers, with the exception of members of collective farms, receive their incomes in the form of wages or salaries. Profits and rents are not paid out as personal incomes, and interest on savings accounts is relatively unimportant. Incomes are spent in state and cooperative stores which charge prices that are set by appropriate authorities or calculated according to prescribed formulas. However, the distribution of real income does not coincide with the distribution of money income. There are two reasons for this. First, there are special shops open only to certain privileged sectors of the population where money spent yields amounts and qualities of goods different from those available to the general public. And second, services such as housing, education, and health care are provided free or at nominal cost but are also distributed on a differential basis to privileged groups and the general public. Needless to say, the groups privileged with respect to services are in general the same as those with access to special shops. Clearly the distribution of real income in Soviet-type societies is considerably more unequal than the distribution of money income. This fact must be taken into account in evaluating their stratification systems.

Another important characteristic of Soviet-type societies is the existence of what is known as a "second" or "underground" economy consisting of the production and buying and selling of goods and services by private individuals outside the channels provided and prescribed by the legal system. There is a considerable literature, mostly of an anecdotal sort, dealing with this phenomenon; but given its generally illegal character, there are of course no official or reliable statistics by which to estimate its size or importance relative to the system as a whole. The activities which it encompasses are numerous and variegated, many and perhaps even most of them involving moonlighting by workers and professionals with regular jobs in the state sector: construction and repair work for individuals and households, doctors treating private patients on the side, buying and selling illegally produced or stolen goods, and so on. To the extent that these activities complement the official economy, which is notoriously deficient in the provision of badly needed repair services, they are generally tolerated. But where they contradict and conflict with the official economy, as in the reportedly widespread activity of dealing in goods stolen from state enterprises, they are proscribed and subjected to extremely severe criminal penalties. In any case, there can be little doubt that the second economy provides a strong stimulant to the spirit of private enterprise and constitutes a fertile breeding ground for corruption at all levels of society.

Up to now every post-revolutionary society has either begun as, or quickly developed into, a one-party state, with the ruling party exercising a monopoly of political power. Why this has been so and whether or not it was inevitable are questions we cannot attempt to answer here. The fact is that it has happened; and unless or until experience points to a different conclusion, we must assume that the one-party system is an integral feature of the post-revolutionary society which we are trying to analyze.

It is well known that traditional Marxist theory has always treated political parties as representatives of social classes or segments of social classes. Is this also applicable to post-revolutionary societies? The answer, in my opinion, is yes, but in a considerably more complex sense than the notion of a simple one-way class/

party relationship might suggest. The case of the Soviet Union, aspects of which have been touched on above (especially in Chapter 7), can serve as an example of the kind of tangled issues involved and of what appears to be the outcome toward which the other post-revolutionary societies are tending.

There is no doubt that the Bolshevik Party, which became the single governing party in the Soviet Union, started as a party of the urban proletariat and as such led the way to the seizure of power in the Russian Revolution. With the decimation and dispersal of this class in the years of civil war, however, the estabished relation between class and party was largely dissolved, and for a number of years (roughly the 1920s and 1930s) the party ruled through its control of the armed forces and the security apparatus but without any clear or consistent class base.

In my opinion the key to understanding Soviet society is the recognition that it was during these years of turmoil and conflict that a new class was born and gradually gained control over the Communist Party, liquidated its old (Bolshevik) leadership, and installed itself as a ruling class in the full sense of the term. The process has been described and analyzed in detail by Charles Bettelheim in the two volumes reviewed in Chapters 4, 5, and 7 above. Here I cite a description by Moshe Lewin, one of the leading Western historians of Soviet society, which brilliantly distills the essence of this crucially important development. Discussing the incredible difficulty of governing an economy and society as huge, backward, and divided as the Soviet Union, Lewin writes:

> The problem was not just one of getting enough specialists and managers. There was the parallel problem of promoting a powerful class of bosses, the different *nachal'stvo*, composed of top managers in the enterprises, and top administrators in state agencies. The *nachal'stvo*, . . . the state's ruling stratum was the key group which the system continued to foster. The rewards for being admitted, especially in a country in a state of penury, were very considerable and the power over subordinates very great. Some of the privileges were openly acknowledged: *personal'naia mashina, personal'naia pensiia* (personal car and special pension) and separate eating places were public knowledge. But much was hidden: for example, closed

supply networks offering goods on *spets-paiki* (special rations); special warrants; a graduated scale of expense accounts and perks; privileged housing; well-sheltered resorts; and, finally, the "sealed envelope" with money over and above the formal salary. All these were slowly developed into a formalized hierarchy of material rewards corresponding to a formally stratified and quite rigid ladder of importance and power.

The *nachal'stvo* class was born from the *edinonachalie* principle (one-man rule), especially as it developed in the work place after 1929. The creation of a hierarchical scaffolding of dedicated bosses, held together by discipline, privilege and power, was a deliberate strategy of social engineering to help stabilize the flux. It was born, therefore, in conditions of stress, mass disorganization and a struggle for order and compliance in a state of social warfare. *Nachal'stvo* members were actually asked to see themselves as commanders in battle. The party wanted the bosses to be efficient, powerful and harsh, and endowed them with prerogatives and appropriate encouragement. It was the top party bosses of the Stalinist school who got results whatever the cost . . . , impetuous and capable of pressurizing ruthlessly, who were the models offered to the growing squad of *nachal'niki* . . . . The promotion of the despotic manager, increasingly the regime's style of leadership, was a process by which not leaders but rulers were formed. The fact that many of them were themselves quite insecure as to their jobs made the despotic traits of their rule probably more rather than less capricious and offensive. Occasional purges of "enemies" within the *nachal'stvo* were probably intended to shake up, destabilize and prevent the hardening of a crust of powerful officials forcing the leadership to recognize their power, and increasing their influence in the state machinery generally. Destabilizing purges, however, did not prevent the *nachal'stvo* from developing a distinct organization, style and "mentality." Shifts of central policy and police raids affected its personnel in the offices, but the impersonal features of a bureaucratic pattern kept coming to the fore. These could be neither purged nor sentenced for "wrecking."[1]

It only needs to be added to complete the picture that after Stalin's departure from the scene the practice of purging the leadership cadres was discontinued. The result was to release this group from the kind of subservience to the party which Stalin had been able to enforce. With this change, the party was in effect transformed from being the master of its top functionaries to being the key instrument through which they exercised their rule over the country.

The question remains whether these bosses—who, as Lewin's analysis makes quite clear, are very far from being mere bureaucrats—constitute a true social class. It is conceivable that they might rather be members of a "power elite" in C. Wright Mills' meaning of the term, i.e., a set of individuals who happen at any given time to occupy the "command posts" of society. In theory such a set of individuals might be recruited from all levels and strata of society, according to criteria of fitness for the functions to be performed. If this were the case, the class composition of the power elite could be heterogenous, perhaps reflecting the class composition of the population as a whole. It is clear, however, that this description does not fit the Soviet power elite at all. True, it was *originally* recruited by the old Bolshevik leadership of the party from various strata of pre-revolutionary society. But with the passage of time and the disappearance of the old leadership, the process changed. Increasingly, the highly privileged and powerful individuals at the top came to see themselves as a body apart, held together (in Moshe Lewin's words) by "discipline, privilege and power" and "developing a distinct organization, style and 'mentality.' " They selected and trained their own replacements, naturally giving preference to young people with life-styles, ideas, and values like their own, which means young people from their own social stratum who were born into a privileged environment and had easy access to the institutions of higher education which increasingly, as in all advanced industrial societies, assumed the task and responsibility of preparing the rising generation for social leadership roles.

What all this adds up to is that a group of disparate individuals summoned to occupy the command posts of Soviet society were gradually shaped through a long series of intense historical experiences into a self-conscious and essentially self-reproducing ruling class. No one understood this process of post-revolutionary class formation better than Mao Tsetung, who fought against it to the best of his ability but in the end unsuccessfully. In 1968 Mao told the French writer André Malraux, "Humanity left to its own devices does not necessarily restore capitalism . . . but it does re-establish inequality. The forces tending toward the creation of new classes are powerful."[2] We can be sure that he was summing up the experience of the two great revolutions of the twentieth century, the Russian as well as the Chinese.

Under capitalism, Marx wrote, "capital and its self-expansion appear as the starting and closing point, [and] production is merely production for capital."[3] This is overwhelmingly the most important fact about capitalist society. Whoever does not grasp it or loses sight of it cannot understand the way capitalism functions, its contradictions and historical limitations. By the same token, the most important difference between capitalism and post-revolutionary society is that this overwhelming dominance of capital has been broken and replaced by the direct rule of a new ruling class which derives its power and privileges not from ownership and/or control of capital but from the, unmediated control of the state and its multiform apparatuses of coercion. This means that the utilization of society's surplus product—which, as under capitalism and some forms of precapitalist society, is produced by a propertyless working class—is no longer governed by the laws of value and capital accumulation but instead becomes the central focus of a political process and of course of political struggles, including (but not exclusively) class struggles. In this respect post-revolutionary societies are unlike capitalism but similar to precapitalist societies which also lack an autonomous economic foundation.

The politicization of the surplus-utilization process has permitted Soviet-type societies to deal effectively (relative to capitalism) with some very basic problems affecting the lives of the masses. The most important of these are employment, education, health, social welfare, and land reform. When appropriate comparisons are made, i.e., between countries with roughly the same per capita incomes (for example, China vs. India or Cuba vs. Mexico), it has been found again and again that the post-revolutionary societies are far ahead in all or most of these fields. The reason has already been alluded to above. The leadership at the time of the revolutionary overthrow of the old society actually represents the exploited and impoverished masses and comes to power on a program of radical socioeconomic reforms which are typically put into effect immediately and as far as existing resources permit. As time passes these reforms are institutionalized: powerful bureaucracies are built around them, and the people come to expect not only their continuation but also their extension and improvement. Eventually even a new ruling class leadership which has little in common with its revolutionary predecessor has to accept them as integral parts of the society over which it presides. Any attempt to cut them back or undermine them would call in question the legitimacy not only of the leadership but of the system itself.

In this sense—and I believe only in this sense—the post-revolutionary societies of our time mark an important historic advance over capitalism. But for most people in the exploited periphery of the global capitalist system, where over half of the world's population still lives, this advance is an enormous stride forward: from death at an early age to a life expectancy approaching the attainable span of the human organism, from semi-starvation to enough to eat, from chronic illness to reasonable health, from illiteracy to the ability to read and write, from grinding insecurity to the peace of mind of a steady job and a pension in old age, in short from a subhuman to at least the beginnings of a human existence. No wonder the example of the post-revolutionary societies has a great appeal for the masses in the Third World. Unless some miracle or catastrophe intervenes, it seems reasonably certain that there will be more revolutions and more post-revolutionary societies in the not distant future.

While the politicization of the surplus-utilization process has enabled post-revolutionary societies to cope with basic problems like unemployment which are endemic even to the most advanced capitalist countries and have reached intolerable proportions in the underdeveloped periphery of the global capitalist system, it cannot be said that the basic contradictions of class society have been eliminated. Indeed, the most fundamental of all these contradictions, the divorce of the real producers of wealth from any meaningful control over what is produced, how it is produced, and to what uses it is put, remains and in some respects has been deepened. The forms in which these contradictions express themselves may have changed, but the substance is still there and continues to give rise to problems and conflicts which in the long run may prove to be as intractable and intolerable as any that beset capitalist society.

This is evidently a vast subject which cannot be satisfactorily outlined, let alone analyzed, in the present context. I want simply to call attention to one aspect which is of growing importance in the Soviet Union and which I believe to be the key to some of the most serious problems which afflict that society.

I have stressed the fact that one of the most important gains of the Russian Revolution was guaranteed employment for workers, that this feature has been, and indeed had to be, retained by the new ruling-class leadership which emerged from the struggles of the 1920s and 1930s, and that it constitutes one of the main attractions of the Soviet-type society for the peoples of the Third World. What needs to be added is that guaranteed employment negates the basic principle of the capitalist incentive system. If workers enjoy tenure and are hence assured of an income, but if the jobs to which they are assigned are boring, debilitating, and degrading—as most work under capitalism is[4]—they will obviously not take an interest in what they are doing and will perform as little work as they can get away with. Capitalism's tried and true remedy for this is unemployment, the threat of which hangs over workers like a sword of Damocles, forcing them to ever greater exertions to avoid being fired and losing their means of livelihood.

The problem for the Soviet Union is that it has removed the sword of Damocles without putting anything in its place. During the early years of industrialization extreme measures of coercion were widely used, including deprivation of housing and food rations and even deportation to labor camps. While this succeeded after a fashion in molding a mass of raw peasants into an industrial proletariat, it did not solve the real problem and was never intended to be permanent. What was needed, as socialists have long contended, was a radically different attitude toward work and workers, involving the workers in decision-making at all levels of the economy and society, and encouraging them to take upon themselves the task of humanizing the work process as the collective responsibility of free men and women. It may be of course that traveling this road was never possible in the circumstances prevailing in the Soviet Union. It could be argued that it would have required the leadership and guidance of a party deeply rooted in the working class and dedicated to its emancipation, and that what might have become such a party was consumed in the flames of civil war. But whether or not this is true—and we shall never know for sure—there can be no doubt that there was never the slightest chance that the new ruling class which emerged later on would opt for a course which, if successful, would lead to full-scale democratization and the loss of its monopoly of power and privileges.

This ruling class, in keeping with what we know about its origins and nature, opted for a very different course, that of depoliticizing the working class, depriving it of all means of self-organization and self-expression, and turning it into a mere instrument in the hands of an increasingly powerful state. It seems to have worked so far (though it cannot be denied that this may be only an appearance based on ignorance), but this "success" has had a very high price. A depoliticized working class not spurred on by a capitalist incentive system (a complex of fears, not only of being fired but also of being demoted, losing income and status, and much more) seems to be a working class which is not much interested in working its head off for goals—catching up with the capitalists, maximizing military power, or whatever—that are established by a ruling class with which it shares little but a long relationship of abuse and oppression.

The result is that the performance of the Soviet economy, even in purely quantitative terms, has for some time now been lagging behind its leaders' ambitions and the potential of its human productive resources. Attempts are being made to turn the situation around by massive imports of capital and sophisticated technology from the advanced capitalist countries, but the real problems are human and social, not technological; and increasing dependence on capitalism, if allowed to go too far, could easily be a source of weakness rather than strength. It would perhaps be too much to say that post-revolutionary society, as represented by its oldest and most advanced exemplar, has reached a dead end.

But at least one can say that it seems to have entered a period of stagnation, different from the stagflation of the advanced capitalist world but showing no more visible signs of a way out.

(February 1980)

NOTES

Chapter 2. Lessons of Poland

1. Isaac Deutscher, *On Socialist Man* (New York: Merit Publishers, 1967), p. 17.
2. *New York Times*, December 14, 1970.
3. Kalecki, *Theory of Economic Dynamics* (New York: Monthly Review Press, 1968), p. 63.
4. Zauberman, *Industrial Progress in Poland, Czechoslovakia, and East Germany, 1937–1962* (London: Oxford University Press, 1964).
5. *New York Times*, December 30, 1970.
6. Nicholas Bethell, *Gomulka: His Poland, His Communism* (New York: Holt, Rinehart and Winston, 1969), pp. 208–209.
7. Quoted in ibid., pp. 217–218.
8. *New York Times*, December 21, 1970.
9. E. Preobrazhensky, *The New Economics* (New York: Oxford University Press, 1965), p. 159.
10. Gurley, "Capitalist and Maoist Economic Development," *Monthly Review* (February 1971), pp. 15–35.
11. The best assessment we have yet seen is that of Bernard Margueritte in *Le Monde*. See "Poland: Wage Increases and No More Double-Think," *Le Monde Weekly* (in English), January 6, 1971, p. 3.

Chapter 3. Transition to Socialism

1. Karl Marx and Friedrich Engels, *Werke*, vol. 4, p. 160.
2. Ibid., vol. 8, p. 142.
3. Writing Group of the Kirin Provincial Revolutionary Committee, "Socialist Construction and Class Struggle in the Field of Economics—Critique of Sun Yeh-fang's Revisionist Economic Theory," *Peking Review*, April 17, 1970, p. 9.
4. Quoted in *Le Monde Weekly*, January 13, 1971, p. 8.
5. Mao Tsetung, *Selected Works*, vol. II, p. 324.
6. *Hongqi*, no. 5 (1964). The brackets are in the original.
7. V. I. Lenin, *Collected Works*, vol. 28, pp. 424–425.
8. Mao Tsetung, *Selected Works*, vol. IV, p. 374.

9. Quoted in the concluding chapter of Jean Daubier, *Histoire de la révolution culturelle prolétarienne en Chine* (Paris: Maspero, 1970).

Chapter 4. The Nature of Soviet Society—1

1. First published in French in 1974. First English-language edition published by Monthly Review Press in 1976, translated by Brian Pearce. All citations are from this edition. The second volume was published in French in 1977 and in English in 1978. The third volume is expected in 1981.
2. Ibid., p. 10.

Chapter 5. The Nature of Soviet Society—2

1. On this, the book by Moshe Lewin, *Lenin's Last Struggle* (New York: Pantheon, 1968), is very revealing. Bettelheim mentions this work but makes less use of it than he well could have.
2. E. H. Carr, *The Bolshevik Revolution, 1917–1923*, vol. 1, p. 224.
3. Charles Bettelheim, *Cultural Revolution and Industrial Organization in China: Changes in Management and the Division of Labor* (New York: Monthly Review Press, 1974), p. 73.
4. Quoted by Bettelheim in ibid., p. 74.
5. Ibid., p. 76.
6. For a discussion of the nature and role of economism, see Chapter 4.

Chapter 6. Theory and Practice in the Mao Period.

1. This problem and its implications are analyzed by Harry Magdoff in an important article, "China: Contrasts with the USSR," *Monthly Review* (July–August 1975), especially pp. 29–32.
2. See the article by Magdoff cited in the previous footnote, and Ben Stavis, "China's Green Revolution," *Monthly Review* (October 1974).

Chapter 7. Bettelheim on Revolution from Above.

1. *Class Struggles in the USSR: Second Period, 1923–1930*, which was first published in French in 1977 and in English by Monthly Review Press in 1978, translated by Brian Pearce.
2. Most important are Sigrid Grosskopf, *L'Alliance ouvrière et paysanne en URSS (1921–1928): Le Problème du blé* (Paris, 1976); and Moshe Lewin, *La Paysannerie et le pouvoir soviétique* (Paris, 1966); English translation, *Russian Peasants and Soviet Power* (Evanston, Ill.: Northwestern University Press, 1968).
3. See particularly the section entitled "The underestimation of the potentialities of the poor and middle peasants' farms," pp. 103–105.
4. Harry Magdoff, "China: Contrasts with the USSR," *Monthly Review* (July–August 1975), pp. 25, 27n.
5. For references see the entries under "Bourgeoisie" in the index.

Chapter 8. Is There a Ruling Class in the USSR?

1. My understanding of this theory comes partly from more than forty years of active interest and participation in discussions and debates over the interpretation of the Soviet experience, and more specifically from three published works: (1) Leon Trotsky, *The Revolution Betrayed* (1937), cited from the 1945 Pioneer Publishers edition; (2) Trotsky, "The U.S.S.R. in War," *The New International*, November 1939; and (3) Ernest Mandel, "On the Nature of the Soviet State," *New Left Review*, no. 108, March–April 1978.
2. For a fuller exposition of this version of the Marxist theory of the state, see Paul M. Sweezy, *The Theory of Capitalist Development* (1942; New York: Monthly Review Press, 1964), ch. 13. I should note, however, that it was presented there, at least by implication, as a theory specifically applicable to advanced capitalism and not as a universal theory of the state.
3. Trotsky, *The Revolution Betrayed*, p. 59.
4. Trotsky, "The U.S.S.R. in War," pp. 326, 327, 329.
5. Mandel, "On the Nature of the Soviet State," p. 43.
6. Ibid., p. 31.
7. A by no means exhaustive list includes *Russia after Stalin* (1953), *Russia in Transition* (1957), and *Ironies of History* (1966). The last-named is a collection of essays containing reprints from the 1957 volume, plus other relevant writings of the same period.
8. Deutscher, *Ironies of History*, pp. 18–19, 21, 24–25.
9. Ibid., p. 25.
10. Il Manifesto, ed., *Pouvoir et opposition dans le sociétés post-révolutionnaires* (Paris: Seuil, 1978), p. 39.
11. Mandel, "On the Nature of the Soviet State," p. 43.
12. Ibid., p. 39.
13. Ibid., p. 30.
14. Ibid., p. 40.
15. On this, see also the discussion in Chapter 10, especially the long quotation from Moshe Lewin.
16. In this connection see Kenzo Mohri, "Marx and 'Underdevelopment,'" *Monthly Review* (April 1979).
17. Especially significant (and symptomatic) was Lenin's article "Better Fewer, But Better," *Pravda* (March 2, 1923), his last published work before his final disabling stroke.

Chapter 9. A Crisis in Marxian Theory

1. Thomas Kuhn, *The Structure of Scientific Revolutions* (Chicago: University of Chicago Press, 1970).

Chapter 10. Post-Revolutionary Society

1. Moshe Lewin, "Society and the Stalinist State," *Social History* (Hull, England) (May 1976), pp. 172–173.
2. Quoted by James Peck, "Revolution Versus Modernization and Revisionism:

A Two-Front Struggle," in Victor Nee and James Peck, eds., *China's Uninterrupted Revolution: From 1840 to the Present* (New York: Pantheon Books, 1975), p. 108.

3. Marx, *Capital,* vol. 3, ch. 15, sect. 2.
4. The most complete and authoritative treatment of this subject is Harry Braverman, *Labor and Monopoly Capital: The Degradation of Work in the Twentieth Century* (New York: Monthly Review Press, 1974).